Nelson C. Parshall

Graded Exercises in Analysis, Synthesis, and false Syntax

Nelson C. Parshall

Graded Exercises in Analysis, Synthesis, and false Syntax

ISBN/EAN: 9783337109202

Printed in Europe, USA, Canada, Australia, Japan

Cover: Foto ©ninafisch / pixelio.de

More available books at **www.hansebooks.com**

WITH AN

EXEMPLIFIED OUTLINE

OF THE

SIFICATION OF SENTEN

AND

CLAUSES,

AND A

DIACRITICAL MA

WITH QUESTIONS.

BY

PARSHALL.

ce, under never f
" Prof. W.

Rochester, N.
ED BY TH
1878.

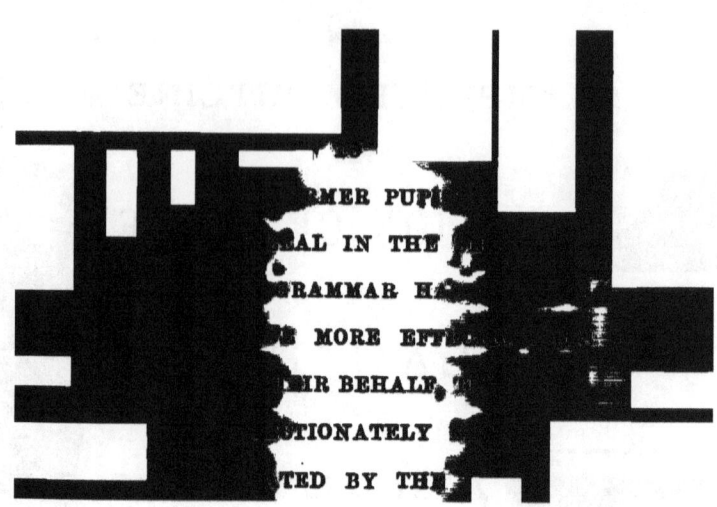

PREFACE.

I. ***The design*** of this book is to supply the long existing need of an Exercise Book to facilitate and make attractive grammatical study. It claims to be neither an English Grammar nor a substitute for one, but is intended as a *practical working book* for the use of all who teach or study the subject.

II. ***Its chief contents*** comprise *fifty graded Exercises*, each of which is divided into three sections. The *first* treats, principally, of *Analysis*, or separating into parts; the *second*, of *Synthesis*, or forming wholes from parts, and the *third*, of *False Syntax*, in which the pupil is required to discern, criticise, and correct the wrong use of language.

III. ***The terms*** employed are such as are in general use in the best text-books on the subject, and for convenience of reference are presented at one view, with many others, under the head of *Equivalent Terms*.

IV. ***The selections*** for Analysis are from the best specimens of English, and have been chosen as well on account of their intrinsic beauty and force, as for their fitness in illustrating the purest diction and idiom of the language.

V. ***Mere parsing,*** as an expert performance, is nearly valueless, and has been superseded by a system of pointed questioning, directed to the salient points *alone*, thus testing and developing the student's knowledge without waste of time. In general, but a single answer is required to each question proposed, which will greatly add to precision in answering the questions, as well as in making up the percentage of results.

VI. ***The grading*** has been made a special object of care, and it is believed that the first Exercise will be found so simple that it may be undertaken by the student almost at the outset of his grammatical course.

VII. ***Synthesis*** is given a co-ordinate place with Analysis as they are in their nature inseparable. All the practical value of Analysis and **Parsing is exemplified** only in the constant **practice of Synthesis**; and yet, **as a systematic study**, Synthesis is unknown in the great majority of schools.

The **Synthetic Exercises** are very copious, and cover the most important points of the entire grammatical course, and serve not only as tests of the student's proficiency in Grammar, but also afford him an excellent drill in practical composition.

VIII. *The False Syntax* has been prepared with great care, mostly from original sources. The aim has been to reflect the common errors as observed in the current speech and literature of the day, while excluding the vulgar slang as well as the excessively fine, and the mooted points of usage.

IX. *An Exemplified Outline* of the Classification of Sentences and Clauses is given, not to teach that subject, but to afford a convenient model of reference for the use of both teacher and pupil.

X. *A Table of Diacritical Marks* with Questions is added as a special feature, which it is hoped will commend itself to teachers generally. This subject, as I believe, has not hitherto appeared in any text-book, as a separate object of study; and that its great importance deserves this distinction, will hardly be questioned, when it is remembered that but few persons can consult a dictionary *intelligently in this respect*.

XI. *These Exercises* have had their inception, their growth, and their completion, in the school room, where they have been tested in the author's own classes with the most satisfactory results.

XII. *This work* is respectfully submitted to my fellow teachers in the hope that it may prove itself a valuable auxiliary in the practical study of English Grammar.

N. C. PARSHALL,
Principal of Wadsworth Grammar School.

Rochester, N. Y., August, 1878.

SOURCE OF SELECTIONS.

WHITTIER.	GRAY.	PLUTARCH.
HUGO.	WILLIS.	CHARLOTTE ELIZABETH.
BLACK HAWK.	BYRON.	MRS. BROWNING.
OSSIAN.	LONGFELLOW.	BUNYAN.
WORDSWORTH.	ANDERSEN.	BEATTIE.
DIMOND.	CAMPBELL.	POPE.
LAMB.	EMERSON.	DRAKE.
MORRIS.	GOLDSMITH.	COWPER.
EVERETT.	SHELLEY.	IRVING.
MRS. HEMANS.	SCOTT.	SHAKSPEARE.
HAWTHORNE.	ÆSOP.	BACON.
CHANNING.	KNOWLES.	ADDISON.
MOORE.	FROM THE GERMAN.	CARLYLE.
DICKENS.	SOCRATES.	MACAULAY.
WOLF.	MILTON.	RUSKIN.
GILPIN.	THACKERAY.	TENNYSON.

A

CLASSIFIED OUTLINE OF SENTENCES.

Tabular View.

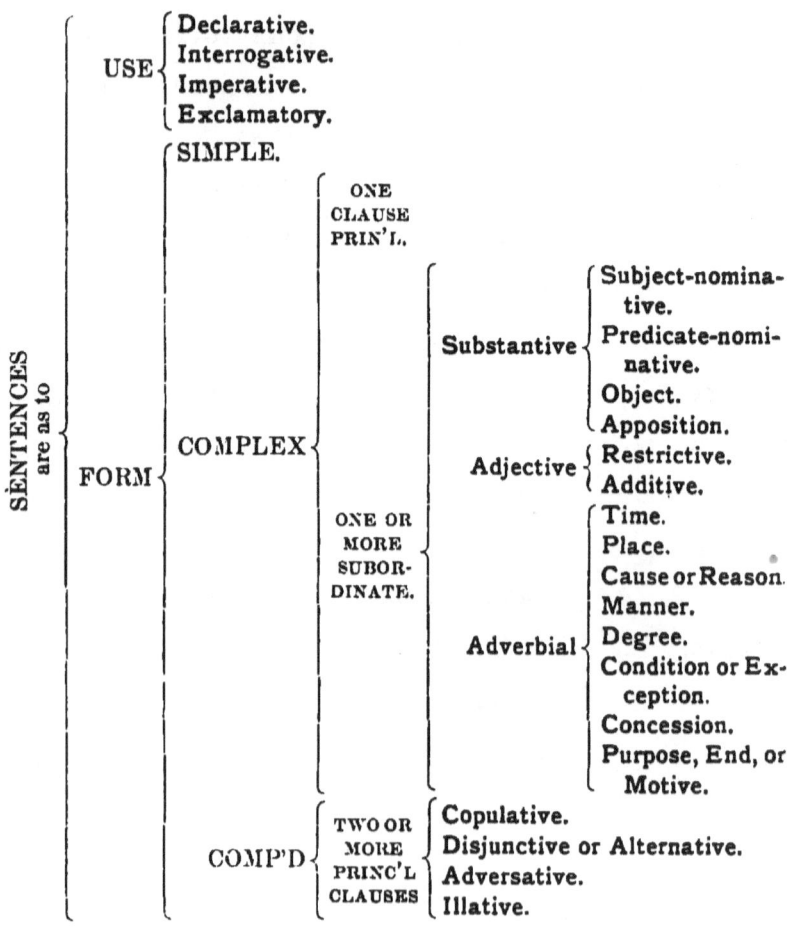

SENTENCES are as to

- USE
  - Declarative.
  - Interrogative.
  - Imperative.
  - Exclamatory.
- FORM
  - SIMPLE. *(ONE CLAUSE PRIN'L.)*
  - COMPLEX *(ONE OR MORE SUBORDINATE.)*
    - Substantive
      - Subject-nominative.
      - Predicate-nominative.
      - Object.
      - Apposition.
    - Adjective
      - Restrictive.
      - Additive.
    - Adverbial
      - Time.
      - Place.
      - Cause or Reason.
      - Manner.
      - Degree.
      - Condition or Exception.
      - Concession.
      - Purpose, End, or Motive.
  - COMP'D *(TWO OR MORE PRINC'L CLAUSES)*
    - Copulative.
    - Disjunctive or Alternative.
    - Adversative.
    - Illative.

EXAMPLES OF SIMPLE SENTENCES.

Words Added.

1. Birds sing. — *Simple subj. and pred.*
2. Bees make *honey*. — *Object.*
3. *Tall* and *beautiful* poplars lined *the* bank. ⎫
4. The air was *soft* and *balmy*. ⎬ *Adjectives.*
5. The blood runs *cold*. ⎪
6. Heat me the iron *hot*. ⎭
7. This is the *forest* primeval. ⎫
8. Tom struts a *soldier*. ⎬ *Pred-nom.*
9. The corporal was chosen *captain*. ⎭
10. I heard the *king's* command. ⎱ *Possessives.*
11. *Our* thoughts, *our* angels are. ⎰
12. Milton, the *poet*, was blind. ⎱ *Appositives.*
13. 'Tis I, *Hamlet* the *Dane*. ⎰
14. *Slowly* and *sadly* they laid him *down*. ⎱ *Adverbs.*
15. They are *now here* studying *very diligently*. ⎰

Phrases Added.

                                                        Simple.

16. The blue face *of ocean* smiled. ⎧ *Prepositional*
17. We saw a noble stag *scaling yonder cliff*. **Adj.** ⎨ *Participial.*
18. Leaves have their time *to fall*. ⎩ *Infinitive.*
19. The dying notes still linger *on the string*. ⎧ *Prepositional.*
20. The waves mount up *to kiss the* **Adv'l.** ⎨ *Infinitive.*
    blushing morn.
21. He fell *grasping his sword*. **Adv.-Adj.** { *Participial.*

EXEMPLIFIED OUTLINE.

Simple.

22. *Toward the rising sun* is called east. — Prepositional
23. *John's sawing wood so fast* is foolish. — Substantive. — Participial.
24. *To be good* is *to be happy.* — Infinitive.
25. *Generally speaking*, it is true. — Independ't. — Participial.
26. *To say truly*, I cannot credit it. — Infinitive.

Complex.

27. He strode haughtily *into the thickest of the group.* — Prepositional
28. *Gaily chattering to the pattering of the brown nuts downward clattering*, leapt the squirrels red and gray. — Participial.
29. The miser strives *to live poor to die rich.* — Infinitive.

Compound

30. The hunters rode *through the meadow and by the mill.* — Prepositional
31. Who can tell the triumph of the mind *By truth illumined and by taste refined?* — Participial
32. The girls once learned *to knit* and *to sew.* — Infinitive.

Compound Principal Parts.

33. There *health* and *plenty* cheered the laboring swain.
34. Twilight *lets* her curtain down and *pins* it with a star.
35. She plucked the *daisies* white and *violets* blue.
36. *Cats* and *dogs* catch and *eat* rats and *mice*.

A Simple Sentence.

The applause of listening senates to command,
  The threats of pain and ruin to despise,
To scatter plenty o'er a smiling land,
  And read their history in a nation's eyes,

Their lot forbade: nor circumscribed alone
 Their glowing virtues, but their crimes confined;
Forbade to wade through slaughter to a throne
 And shut the gates of mercy on mankind;

The struggling pangs of conscious truth to hide,
 To quench the blushes of ingenuous shame,
Or heap the shrine of Luxury and Pride
 With incense kindled at the Muse's flame.
GRAY'S ELEGY.

COMPLEX SENTENCES

CONTAINING

Adjective Clauses.

1. The **man** *who feels truly noble* will become so.
2. He was a **man** *of whom the world was not worthy.*
3. **Those** *that think* must govern **those** *that toil.*
4. I will assist such **pupils** *as require my aid.*
5. Happy and worthiest of esteem are **those**
    whose words are bonds, whose oaths are oracles.
6. **He** *who buys the things which he does not need*
    will often need the **things** *which he can not buy.*
7. **THAT** / **WHICH** *reason weaves* is undone by passion¹.
8. The metal is not **THAT** / **WHICH** *it was supposed to be.*
9. We cannot cure *what we must endure.*

---

¹ Some grammarians treat "*What reason weaves*," and similar constructions, as *substantive clauses.*

10. Whoever is so anxious with respect to what he is charged with, as not to mind what others are doing, or have to do, is what might be called a sensible man.
11. Whatever purifies, fortifies also the heart.
12. Whosoever will, may come.
13. Whatsoever he doeth, shall prosper.
14. Give it to whomsoever you may select.
15. The gentleman kindly lent what money was required.
16. *Who steals my purse*, steals trash.
17. **His** praise is lost *who waits for all to commend.*
18. The **bill was rejected** by the Lords, *which excited much comment.*
19. The lad **tells the truth,** *which you do not.*
20. The servant is **faithful,** *which you are not.*
21. I know a **bank** *whereon the wild thyme grows.*
22.   Those that fly may fight again,
      Which he can never do that's slain.
23.   Not a soldier discharged his farewell shot
      O'er the **grave** *where our hero was buried.*
24. All claims, *whatever their nature may be,* are referred to the committee.
25. **All claims,** *of whatever nature they may be,* are referred to the committee.

RESTRICTIVE.

26. The **evil** *that men do* lives after them.

Note.—The antecedent of the relative is usually preceded by some limiting word; as, *a, an, the,* or *that.*

ADDITIVE.

27. A glass was offered to **Mannering,** *who drank it to the health of the reigning prince.*
28. I thrice presented him a kingly **crown,** *which he did thrice refuse.*
29. The servant **closed the blinds,** *which darkened the room.*

Note.—See examples 18, 19, 20 and 22, above.

EXEMPLIFIED OUTLINE.

COMPLEX SENTENCES

CONTAINING

Substantive Clauses.

1. *That you have wronged me,* doth appear in this.
2. How $\begin{Bmatrix} that, when, \\ where, why, \end{Bmatrix}$ *an acorn becomes an oak,* is a mystery.
3. *Can he hold the fort?* is the question.
4. The opinion is, *that the moon is not inhabited.*
5. We cannot tell *how (when, where, why,) an acorn becomes an oak.*
6. The footman, in his usual phrase,
   Comes up with, *"Madam, dinner stays."*
7. The hope *that he might win the prize* greatly stimulated him.
8. It is well known *that the Egyptians embalmed their dead.*
9. See *what a rent the envious Casca made.*
10. One truth is clear, *whatever is, is right.*
11. *What reason weaves,* by passion is undone.¹

COMPLEX SENTENCES

With **Adverbial Clauses** referring to

TIME.

1. They kneeled *before* $\begin{Bmatrix} when, while, whilst, \\ as, after, ere, till, \\ until, since, whenever, \\ as\ soon\ as, as\ often\ as, \\ as\ long\ as, \end{Bmatrix}$ *they fought.*

---

¹ See No. 7, complex sentences containing adjective clauses.

PLACE.

2. Go { *where, wherever, whither, whithersoever, as far as, whence,* } *glory waits thee.*

CAUSE OR REASON.

3. As { *because, whereas, since, inasmuch as, seeing that,* } *Cæsar loved me,* I weep for him.
4. Rise, *for the day is breaking.*
5. I am proud *that I am an American.*

MANNER—*by Comparison.*

6. He lived *as mothers wish their sons to live.*
7. *As you speak,* so should you think.
8. The honey-bee builds its cells *just as it did at first.*
9. The beaver built his dam at first as well *as he does to-day.*
10. I will shoot three arrows on this side { *as though as if,* } *I shot at a mark.*
11. The little girl acted as bravely *as her brother.*
12. The nightingale sings better *than the thrush.*

By Effect.

13. The young man acts so, *that all his friends are proud of him.*
14. The conditions were so expressed, *that they were accepted at once.*

By relating to the assertion in the nature of a modal adverb.

15. It was, *as I have said,* a fine autumnal day.
16. He returned, *as he told me,* on the last steamer.
17. She praised the singing of the young rustic, *as she called him.*

DEGREE—*By Comparison.*

18. That maple is as tall *as that oak.*
19. The pine is taller *than the oak.*

EXEMPLIFIED OUTLINE. 15

20. The maple is more beautiful *than the oak.*
21. *As Washington is loved for his patriotism,* so Arnold is despised for his treachery.
22. Hampden was as good *as he was great.*
23. Some men are loved for their benevolence, *as others are despised for their selfishness.*
24. *The higher up the mountain we climb,* the cooler will be the air.
25. *The deeper the well,* the cooler the water.

Note.—By expanding the above, the principal proposition becomes apparent: The water is cooler *in the degree in which* the well is deeper. *The cooler* = cooler in the degree. *The deeper* = deeper in which. Strike out the reciprocal adjectives and *The* = in the degree. *The* = in which.

By Effect.

26. The night was so cold, *that water froze in the buckets.*
27. The terms of the treaty were such, *that they were accepted at once.*

CONDITION OR EXCEPTION.

28. *If I were not Alexander,* I would be Diogenes.
29. *Were I not Alexander,* I would be Diogenes.
30. I will go *provided you remain.*
31. *Except I be by Silvia by night,* there is no music in the nightingale.
32. The vessel will be lost *unless the storm abates.*
33. *Could we ascend the mountain,* a beautiful sight would greet us.
34. *Is any one in want,* charity shall relieve him.

CONCESSION.

35. *Though the man is poor,* he is wise and honorable.
36. *Though (although) he slay me* { *yet, still, nevertheless,* } I will trust in Him.

37. { *Whoever* / *Whatever* } *may oppose that man*, he is sure to succeed.
38. *However he is baffled*, the general is always hopeful of victory.
39. *However powerful may be the enemy*, he cannot take the fort.
40. *Poor as the young man was*, he gave most liberally to the cause.

PURPOSE, END, OR MOTIVE.

41. Awake your senses *that you may the better judge.*
42. Love not sleep *lest thou come to poverty.*
43. Regulus gave up his life *in order that Rome might be saved.*
44. We have been the more careful, *that we might not do him an injustice.*

A Complex Sentence.

45. If the constitution of our state, now and always, has declared that no right of conscience, and no form or mode of religious worship, shall be controlled or interfered with, and requires, in offices of the highest trust, no religious qualification but a belief in the existence of a Supreme Being, and His power to punish or reward our actions, we proudly remember that this glorious principle is foremost in the earliest of our laws, voluntarily proclaimed by Penn before he left the shores of England ; and that he, among all legislators, was the first to guarantee, by the enactments of his civil code, the full enjoyment of this Christian liberty to every one living in his province, " who should confess and acknowledge one Almighty God to be the creator, upholder, and ruler of the world."

H. D. GILPIN.

COMPOUND SENTENCES.
Copulative Clauses.

1. The vine still clings to the mouldering wall,
   And at every gust the dead leaves fall.
2. The maidens left their weaving;
   The lads forgot their play.
3. *Not only* was the division repulsed *but* the entire corps was routed.
4. The young man, *as well as* his friends, was hopeful.
5. The lady is a fine artist; *furthermore*, she sings beautifully.
6. I really do not sing; *besides*, I have a cold.
7. The rain came down in torrents; *moreover*, the bridge was not safe.
8. The terrific flashes of lightning and the heavy claps of thunder frightened the women quite out of their wits; *even*, (*likewise, also,*) the men were far from being unmoved.
9. The fort was taken by storm; *and* that, too, without the loss of a single man.

Disjunctive or Alternative.

1. For them no more the blazing hearth shall burn,
   Or busy housewife ply her evening care.
2. We cannot go, *nor* should you.
3. *Either* you must submit, *or* I shall dismiss you.
4. Yield, *or else* I'll hew thee piece-meal.
5. You must study hard; *otherwise* a failure will be the result.

Adversative.

1. I go *but* I return.
2. I have but little faith; *however*, I will make the effort.

3. His offence was very grave; *yet,* { *still, nevertheless, notwithstanding,* } I am inclined to overlook it.
4. He is a talented man; *though* he does not seem so.
5. He would be a soldier; *only* he is too young.

Illative.

1. The fort is yours, *then* defend it.
2. The angles are equal; *therefore* the sides are equal.
3. He blushes; *and hence* he is guilty.
4. The morning was dark and rainy, *so* we remained at home.
5. Showers come frequently; *consequently,* the grass grows rapidly.
6. The soil is rich; *accordingly,* the trees grow tall.
7. The moon is very bright, *and so* I shall remain longer.
8. The storm is abroad in the mountain; *wherefore,* it will soon sweep over the valley.

A Compound Sentence.

The mountain wooded to the peak, the lawns
And winding glades high up like ways to Heaven,
The slender coco's drooping crown of plumes,
The lightning flash of insect and of bird,
The lustre of the long convolvuluses
That coiled around the stately stems, and ran
Ev'n to the limit of the land, the glows
And glories of the broad belt of the world,
All these he saw; but what he fain had seen
He could not see, the kindly human face,
Nor ever hear a kindly voice, but heard
The myriad shriek of wheeling ocean-fowl,
The league-long roller thundering on the reef,
The moving whisper of huge trees that branch'd

And blossom'd in the zenith, or the sweep
Of some precipitous rivulet to the wave,
As down the shore he ranged, or all day long
Sat often in the seaward-gazing gorge,
A shipwrecked sailor, waiting for a sail;
No sail from day to day, but every day
The sunrise broken into scarlet shafts
Amoug the palms and ferns and precipices;
The blaze upon the waters to the east;
The blaze upon his island overhead;
The blaze upon the waters to the west;
Then the great stars that globed themselves in Heaven,
The scarlet shafts of sunrise—but no sail.
TENNYSON, *Enoch Arden.*

EXAMPLES OF SENTENCES

CLASSIFIED ACCORDING TO

USE.

Declarative.

1. A mist rose slowly from the lake.

Interrogative.

2. *Is* your name Shylock?
3. *Who* was the author of Junius's letters?
4. *How* does an acorn become an oak?
5. You find it strange, sir?
6. *Art* thou he that should come, or *do* we look for another?
7. *Is* it amusing? you find it strange?

Imperative.

8. Heat me the iron hot.

Exclamatory.

9. How sweet the moonlight sleeps upon this bank!
10. What sad scenes were once enacted here!
11. How could you be so cruel!
12. Quit the bust above my door!
13. How merrily the waves dance on! and how beautiful they all appear!

Declarative-Interrogative.

14. So Heaven decrees; with Heaven who can contend?

Declarative-Imperative.

15. Act well thy part; there all the honor lies.

Declarative-Exclamatory.

16. The lights burn blue; how dreadful is this place!

Exclamatory-Interrogative.

17. From the vale on they come! and will ye quail?

Imperative-Interrogative.

Bid every man on deck; and the skipper, where is he?

Exclamatory-Imperative.

19. How wondrously beautiful is the night! then let us hasten on our journey.

Table of Diacritic Marks.

The Macron (¯).
1. ā long as in āle.
2. ē long as in ēat.
3. ī long as in īce.
4. ō long as in ōld.
5. ū long as in ūse.
6. ȳ long as in mȳ.
7. ẹ as in thẹy, hẹinous.
8. o͞o as in mo͞on.
9. g̱ as in g̱et.
10. ṉ as in liṉger, iṉk.
11. th as in thine.
12. c hard as in cap.
13. ch as in echo.

The Breve (˘).
1. ă short as in ăt.
2. ĕ short as in ĕnd.
3. ĭ short as in ĭnk.
4. ŏ short as in ŏn.
5. ŭ short as in ŭp.
6. y̆ short as in nby̆ss.
7. o͝o short as in go͝od.

The Dieresis (¨).
1. ä as in fär.
2. ạ as in ạll.
3. ï like long e, as in police.
4. ö like long oo, as in dö.
5. ṳ preceded by r, as in rṳde.

The Period (·).
1. ȧ as in ȧsk.
2. ạ as in whạt.
3. ȯ like short u, as in lȯve.
4. ọ like short oo, as in wọlf.
5. ṳ like short oo as in pṳll.
6. ġ soft like j, as in ġem.

The Circumflex (^).
1. â as in câre, âir.
2. ê like a in câre, as in êre.
3. ô like a in all, as in ôrb.
4. û as in ûrge.

The Cedilla (̧).
1. ç soft like s, as in çede.
2. çh like sh, as in çhaise.

(̣).
1. ẓ like z, as in haẓ.
2. x̣ like gz, as in ex̣ist.

The Tilde (~).
1. õ as in hẽr.
2. ĩ like ẽ, as in ãir.

Equivalents.
ā as in āle = ẹ as in thẹy.
â as in âir = ê as in êre.
ạ as in ạll = ô as in ôrb.
ē as in ēve = ï as in police.
ẽ as in vẽrge = ĩ as in ãir.
ọ as in dọ = ṳ as in rṳle = o͞o as in mo͞on.
ạ as in whạt = ŏ as in nŏt.
ĭ as in ĭt = y̆ as in by̆mn.
ọ as in wọlf = ṳ as in pṳt = o͝o as in bo͝ok.
ȯ as in lȯve = ŭ as in lŭck.

NOTE 1. The **Tilde** is placed over some Spanish words, as cañon, to indicate that, in pronunciation, the sound of the following vowel is to be preceded by that of initial y.

NOTE 2. Those consonants whose sounds are indicated by a *short, straight, horizontal* mark, are placed under the head of the *macron*, although strictly speaking, its use is confined to the *long* sound of the vowels.

Questions on the Table of Diacritical Marks.

1. Write a word containing the long or name sound of a *properly marked*.
2. Properly mark the sound of a as in **cat**.
3. Of a as in **far**.
4. Of a as in **call**.
5. Of a as in **glass**.
6. Of a as in **share**.
7. Of a as in **what**.
8. Write a word containing the long or name sound of e *properly marked*.
9. Properly mark the sound of e as in **met**.
10. Of e as in **her**.
11. Write a word containing the long or name sound of i *properly marked*.
12. Properly mark the sound of i as in **in**.
13. Write a word containing the long or name sound of o *properly marked*.
14. Properly mark the sound of o as in **on**.
15. Of o as in **do**.
16. Of o as in **wolf**.
17. Write a word containing the long or name sound of u *properly marked*.
18. Properly mark the sound of u as in **up**.
19. Of u as in **full**.
20. Of u as in **rude**.
21. Properly mark the sound of y as in **my**.
22. Of y as in **abyss**.
23. Of e as in **they**.
24. Of i as in **police**.
25. Of oo as in **good**.
26. Of i as in **sir**.
27. Of g as in **get**.

28. Of n as in ink.
29. Of oo as in moon.
30. Of o as in orb.
31. Of u as in urge.
32. Of th as in thy.
33. Of c as in cat.
34. Of c as in cell.
35. Of o as in shove.
36. Of ch as in chaise.
37. Of s as in has.
38. Of g as in gem.
49. Of x as in exist.
40. Of e as in ere.
41. Of ch as in echo.

Write ten words illustrating the use of the *macron* [¯].
Ten of the *breve* [˘].
Ten of the *diæresis* [¨].
Ten of the *period* [·].
Ten of the *cedilla* [ʼ].
Ten of the *circumflex* [^].
Ten of the ——— [˙].
Ten of the *tilde* [˜].

Properly *syllabicate* and *accentuate* the following words and indicate by *diacritic marks* their elementary sounds:

1. Army,
2. alspice,
3. idiocy,
4. ambuscade,
5. careless,
6. emerge,
7. inveigh,
8. asking,
9. what-not,
10. useful,
11. irrefragable,
12. psychology,
13. abyss,
14. benison,
15. heinous,
16. acoustics,
17. machine,
18. exact,
19. thyself,
20. technic,
21. shovel,
22. wolfishness,
23. intercede,
24. post-chaise,
25. finger,
26. ruminate,
27. gingerly,

28. herself,
29. Alabama,
30. zoology,
31. wiseacre,
32. canon (a deep gorge),
33. vaccinate,
34. beneath,
35. tripartite,
36. squalor,
37. sacrifice,
38. acclimate,
39. aeronaut,
40. allopathy,
41. ally,
42. apricot,
43. extol,
44. aureola,
45. borealis,
46. Calliope,
47. coadjutant,
48. combatant,
49. donative,
50. semi-centenary.

EQUIVALENT TERMS.

Entire,
Logical,
Complex,
Modified,
Enlarged,
Complete,
General,
} **Subject or Predicate.**

SUBJECT-NOMINATIVE.
Grammatical,
Simple,
Unmodified,
Bare,
Naked,
Special,
} **Subject or Predicate.**
PREDICATE-VERB.

The term SUBJECT is sometimes applied to the *Subject-nominative* only, and sometimes to the *entire subject expression*.

The term PREDICATE is sometimes applied to the *Verb* alone, and sometimes to the *entire predicate expression*.

SUBSTANTIVE means like, or having the use or value of, a *noun*.

Syntactical Relation,
Syntactical Office,
Syntax,
Office,
Construction,
Disposition,
} **of an element.**

Adjunct,
Modifier,
Qualifier,
Limiter,
} **of an element.**

Modified, Qualified, Limited,	} element.	Present Perfect, Prior Present, Perfect,	}
Properties, Modifications, Accidents, Attributes, Inflections,	} of certain words.	Past Perfect, Prior Past, Pluperfect,	}
		Future-Perfect, Prior Future, Second-Future,	} TENSE.
Infinitive, Infinitive Mood,	} Participle, Participial Mood,	Past, Imperfect,	}
Co-ordinate, Independent, Principal,	} Subordinate, Dependent, Auxiliary, Accessory,	Future, First-future,	}
Present, Imperfect,	} Participle.	Past, Perfect,[1]	} Participle.
	Compound Perfect, Prior Present, Preperfect, Perfect,[1]	} Participle.	

Note to Teachers.

Although Analysis, Synthesis, and False Syntax comprise but a single Exercise, it is not intended that all these subjects should *necessarily* be given as a single lesson.

Each subject is complete in itself, and may be pursued separately, or otherwise, according to the ability, or the degree of advancement, of each class.

---

[1] Grammarians differ widely in classifying the participles.

EXERCISE I.

1. Bees hummed.
2. The sweet song died.
3. The lilies blossom in the pond.
4. The gray sky wears again its gold.
5. The long bright days of summer swiftly passed.
Whittier.

Analysis.

1. Define *English Grammar*.
2. Define a *sentence*.
3. How many *sentences*, or *periods*, in the above Exercise?
4. Of what is something said in the first sentence?
5. What is said of "*bees*"?
6. How many *principal parts* must every sentence have?
7. What is the general name of that part of which something is said?
8. What is the general name of that part which makes the *assertion*?
9. Have the *principal* parts any *modifiers* in the first sentence?
10. What part of speech is "*bees*"?
11. What part of speech is "*hummed*"?
12. Name the *entire* (or *logical*) *subject* of the second sentence.
13. Name the *predicate-verb* (*grammatical predicate*).
14. Name the *subject-nominative* (*grammatical subject*).
15. What two modifiers has the *subject-nominative*?
16. Give the part of speech of "*the*."
17. Of "*sweet*." 18. Of "*song*." 19. Of "*died*."
20. Give the *entire* (or *complex*) *subject* of the third sentence.
21. Give the *entire* (or *complex*) *predicate*.

28 EXERCISES.

22. Give the *subject-nominative* (*simple subject*).
23. What *modifier* has the *subject-nominative?*
24. Give the *predicate-verb* (*simple predicate*).
25. What words tell *where* "*lilies blossom*"?
26. Give the part of speech of "*lilies.*"
27. Of "*blossom.*" 28. Of "*in.*" 29. Of "*pond.*"
30. What is the *entire* (or *logical*) *subject* of the *fourth* sentence?
31. What is the *entire* (or *logical*) *predicate?*
32. What is the *subject-nominative* (*grammatical subject*)?
33. What is the *predicate-verb* (*grammatical predicate*)?
34. By what words is the *subject-nominative* modified?
35. What does "*again*" modify?
36. What word is the *object* of the verb "*wears*"?
37. What *limiting* word has this *object?*
38. Give the part of speech of "*again.*" 39. Of "*its.*"
40. What is the *entire* (or *modified*) *subject* of the last sentence?
41. What is the *entire* (or *modified*) *predicate?*
42. What is the *subject-nominative* (*unmodified subject*)?
43. What is the *predicate-verb* (*verb unmodified*)?
44. Mention the *word* modifier of "*days.*"
45. Mention the *phrase* modifier.
46. What *modifier* has the *predicate-verb?*
47. Give the part of speech of "*long.*"
48. Of "*of.*" 49. Of "*swiftly.*" 50. Of "*passed.*"

Synthesis.

1. Write a sentence containing only a *simple subject* and *predicate*.
2. Add to this sentence an *adjective*.
3. To the sentence last formed, add an *adverb*.
4. Compose a sentence containing an *object* of a verb.
5. Combine *all* the above elements into one sentence.
6. Write a sentence with a word containing an *improper* diphthong *underscored*.
7. One containing a *proper* diphthong.
8. Write a sentence containing a word in which "*w*" is a consonant, and underscore the letter.

9. One containing a word in which "*y*" is a *consonant*.
10. Write in a sentence a word having *two liquids*, and *underscore* the word.
11. Write a sentence of three words, a *monosyllable*, a *dissyllable*, and a *trisyllable*.
12. One containing a *primitive*, a *derivative*, and a *compound* word.
13. Compose a sentence having a *proper noun* subject.
14. A sentence with a *subject* and an *object*, each modified by an *article*.
15. A sentence containing a *preposition*.

False Syntax.[1]

(*Pupils should be required in every case to give a proper reason for the correction.*)

1. I am awful glad.
2. Please can I go out?
3. Aint you afraid you'll catch cold?
4. I despise, not the giver, but gift.
5. He is entitled to the name of a scholar.
6. I'll rant as well as him.
7. Whom besides myself do you think was rewarded?
8. The book is from my brother, he that owns a bookstore.
9. This phenomena appears nightly.
10. These minutiæ is distracting.

[1] The term "*False Syntax*," although not *strictly* applicable to all cases of faulty English, has been retained, as it is a customary and convenient expression to denote the *general* errors in the use of language.

EXERCISE II.

1. Some hours passed.
2. The sun rose in an unclouded sky.
3. Its first ray shone upon a motionless form.
4. It was Gilliatt.
5. He was still outstretched upon the rock.
6. His closed eye-lids were wan.

Victor Hugo.

Analysis.

1. How many *sentences* in the above Exercise?
2. How many *propositions?*
3. Define a *proposition.*
4. What is the *entire subject* of the first proposition?
5. What is meant by the term "*entire subject*"?
6. What word expresses what is said of "*hours*"?
7. What word modifies "*hours*"?
8. Is the second sentence *simple*, or *compound?*
9. Define the class to which you assign this sentence.
10. What is its *entire* (or *enlarged*) *subject?*
11. What is its *entire* (or *enlarged*) *predicate?*
12. What is its *subject-nominative (bare subject)?*
13. What *word modifier* has the subject?
14. What *phrase modifier* has the predicate-verb?
15. Name the modifiers of "*sky.*"
16. Why is "*an*" used before "*unclouded*," rather than "*a*"?
17. Select a *preposition* from the second sentence.
18. Select an *adjective* from it.
19. Is the *third* sentence *simple*, or *compound?*
20. What are its *chief*, or *principal* parts?

EXERCISES. 31

21. By what is the *subject* modified?
22. By what is the *predicate-verb* modified?
23. What *derivative* word in the third sentence?
24. Define a *derivative* word.
25. Give the *subject-nominative* of the fourth sentence.
26. Give its *entire predicate*.
27. Give its *predicate-verb*.
28. What *proper noun* does this sentence contain?
29. Of what *gender* is this noun?
30. Is the fifth sentence *simple*, or *compound?*
31. Give its *simple subject*.
32. Give its *entire predicate*.
33. Give its *predicate-verb*.
34. What *word modifier* has the *predicate verb?*
35. What *phrase modifier?*
36. Give the part of speech of "*he.*" 37. Of "*was outstretched.*"
38. Of "*still.*" 39. Of "*upon.*" 40. Of "*rock.*"
41. Is the last sentence *simple*, or *compound?*
42. Give its *subject-nominative*.
43. Give its *predicate-verb*.
44. What *possessive word* relating to "*eye-lids"?*
45. What *other modifier* coming *before* it, has "*eye-lids"?*
46. What one coming *after* it?
47. For what *noun* does *his* stand?
48. What *compound* word has the *last* sentence?
49. Why does the word "*his*" begin with a capital letter?
50. Give the *rule* requiring "*Gilliatt*" to begin with a capital.

Synthesis.

Write in separate sentences and indicate by the *underscore*, the following:
 1. A *common* noun, *singular* number.
 2. A *collective* noun. 3. An *abstract* noun.
 4. A *verbal*, or *participial* noun.
 5. A *phrase* used as a noun.
 6. A *clause* used as a noun.
 7. A *pronoun* used as a noun.

8. A *letter* used as a noun.
9. A mere *sign* used as a noun.
10. A *proper* noun used as a *common* noun.
11. A *common* noun used as a *proper* noun.
12. A word in which "*u*" is a *consonant*.
13. A word in which "*i*" is a *consonant*.
14. A word containing a *silent* consonant.
15. A word containing a *silent* vowel.

False Syntax.

1. This is an hard task.
2. The soldiers slept in a open field.
3. You and me cannot agree.
4. Them that seek wisdom shall find it.
5. John and him have just returned.
6. I was presented to Mrs. Brown, she that was Miss Smith.
7. I was with my old friends, they whom you saw last summer.
8. Those kind of people will never succeed.
9. Problems of these sort are very easy to solve.
10. We sat beside that smoking embers.

EXERCISE III.

1. Gilliatt looked up.
2. The silence was still profound.
3. The sun disappeared suddenly.
4. The rising cloud had just reached it.
5. Sheets of clouds undulated like folds of giant flags.

Victor Hugo.

Analysis.

1. How many *sentences* in the above Exercise?
2. Give a *proper reason* for your answer.
3. What is the *subject* of the first sentence?
4. Give its *entire predicate*; 5. its *predicate-verb*.
6. What modifier has the *predicate?*
7. What part of speech is "*Gilliatt*"? 8. "*Looked*"? 9. "*Up*"?
10. Classify the second sentence as *simple, complex,* or *compound.*
11. Classify the same as *declarative, interrogative, imperative,* or *exclamatory.*
12. Give its *entire subject;* 13. its *entire predicate.*
14. Give its *subject-nominative;* 15. its *predicate-verb.*
16. Give the *modifier* of the subject.
17. Name the *predicate-adjective.*
18. What does "*still*" modify?
19. Select from this sentence a word containing a *proper diphthong.*
20. Define a *diphthong.* 21. Define a *proper* diphthong.
22. Classify the third sentence *in full* as in 10 and 11.
23. Give its *entire subject;* 24. its *entire predicate.*
25. Give its *subject-nominative;* 26. its *predicate-verb.*
27. Give the modifier of the *subject.*
28. Give the modifier of the *predicate-verb.*

EXERCISES.

29. Select a word having both a *prefix* and a *suffix*.
30. Classify the fourth sentence *in full*.
31. Give its *entire subject;* 32. its *entire predicate.*
33. Give its *subject-nominative;* 34. its *predicate-verb.*
35. Give its *object.*
36. What modifiers has the *subject ?*
37. What does "*just*" modify ? 38. Classify the *last* sentence.
39. Name its *subject-nominative;* 40. its *predicate-verb.*
41. By what is the *subject* modified ?
42. What *phrase-modifier* has the verb ?
43. Give the *word-modifier* of the verb, if any.
44. What does "*of giant flags*" modify ?
45. What modifier has "*flags*"?
46. Give the part of speech of "*sheets.*"
47. Of "*clouds.*" 48. Of "*like.*" 49. Of "*giant.*" 50. Of "*flags.*"

Synthesis.

Write in separate sentences and indicate by the *underscore* the following :

1. A noun in the *first* person by *apposition.*
2. A noun in the *second* person by *apposition.*
3. A noun in the *third* person by *apposition.*
4. A word illustrating the rule for *doubling* the final consonant.
5. A plural noun formed by adding *s* to the singular.
6. One by adding *es* to the singular.
7. A noun having both a *regular* and an *irregular* plural.
8. *Court-martial* in the *plural* number.
9. *Hanger-on* in the *plural* number.
10. *Cupful* in the *plural* number.
11. + in the *plural* number.
12. A word illustrating the rule for *dropping e final.*
13. A word in which it is necessary to *retain e final* to keep *c* or *g* soft.
14. A word in which *e final* is retained to preserve the *identity* of the word.
15. A word in which *e final* is retained before a suffix beginning with a *consonant.*

False Syntax.

1. Thackeray was a greater writer than an artist.
2. An Article is a *the*, an *an*, or an *a*.
3. Nouns have two numbers, the singular and plural.
4. Who took my pencil? Not me, but her.
5. Truth is greater than us all.
6. Who were playing in the park? Us boys.
7. How can you thus address me, I, who am your friend?
8. The cars ran twenty mile an hour.
9. Every one should inform their mind.
10. Nobody should praise themselves.

EXERCISE IV.

1. That was the last sun that shone on Black Hawk. His
2. heart is dead and no longer beats quick in his bosom. He
3. is now a prisoner to the white man. They will do with
4. him as they wish. But he can stand torture and is not
5. afraid of death. He is no coward. Black Hawk is an
6. Indian.

Black Hawk.

Analysis.

1. How many *sentences* in the above extract?
2. How many *clauses?* 3. How many *propositions?*
4. Select a sentence having a *compound* predicate.
5–11. Classify each sentence, as *simple, complex,* or *compound*.
12. Give the *subject* of the *first* sentence.
13. Give its *entire predicate.*
14. Give the *predicate-verb* of the *principal* clause.
15. Give the *predicate-nominative.*
16. By what is this *nominative* modified?

17. Name the *connective* of this sentence.
18. What *part of speech* is this connective?
19. Select an *adjective* phrase; 20. an *adverbial* phrase.
21. Select a *predicate adjective.*
22. Select a *conjunction*, and state what it connects.
23. Select a *preposition* and give the *terms* connected by it.
24. Select a pronoun in the *nominative* case.
25. One in the *possessive* case,
26. And one in the *objective* case.
27. Select an *adverb of negation.*
28. What *proper* noun is used as a *predicate-nominative?*
29. Give the *part of speech* of "*last.*" 30. Of "*shone.*" 31. Of "*dead.*"
32. Of "*no,*" second line. 33. Of "*longer.*" 34. Of "*quick.*"
35. Of "*as.*"
36. Of "*wish.*" 37. Of "*afraid.*" 38. Of "*no,*" fifth line.
39. Of "*coward.*"
40. What does "*in his bosom*" modify?
41. What does "*to the white man*" modify?
42. What does "*with him*" modify?
43. Is "*of death,*" *adjective*, or *adverbial* in office?
44. Name a verb in the *potential mood.*
45. Name a verb in the *future tense.*
46. Change the last sentence to its *corresponding interrogative* use.
47. Give the antecedent of "*they,*" if it has one.
48. Define a *word;* 49. a *syllable;* 50. a *polysyllable.*

Synthesis.

1. Write a *simple declarative* sentence.
2. Change it into an *interrogative* sentence.
3. Change it into an *imperative* sentence.
4. Change it into an *exclamatory* sentence.
5. Write a sentence containing an *article*, an *adjective*, a *noun*, and a *verb.*
6. Add to this sentence a *preposition* and its *object.*
7. Write a sentence containing an *interjection.*

Illustrate in separate sentences the following suggested rules for the use of capitals.
8. The first word of every sentence.
9. The first word of every line of poetry.
10. The first word of a *direct* quotation.
11. A word denoting the Deity.
12. A *proper name* and a *title*.
13. A *proper adjective*.
14. A *personified noun*.
15. The name of a *month* and a *day of the week*.

False Syntax.

1. One horse, a black and a white one, was saddled.
2. Cromwell was styled a Protector.
3. A black and white boy were walking together.
4. Whom do you suppose will come?
5. Dids't thou not say thou and thee were enemies?
6. Him remaining at the fort, we returned.
7. Can you forgive us girls, us who were so forgetful?
8. Passing rich, with forty pound a year.
9. This five and twenty years have I been with you.
10. Damon and Pythias loved one another.

EXERCISE V.

1. Daughter of heaven, fair art thou!
2. The silence of thy face is pleasant!
3. Thou comest forth in loveliness.
4. The stars attend thy blue course in the east.
5. The clouds rejoice in thy presence, O moon!
6. They brighten their dark brown sides.
7. Who is like thee in heaven, light of the silent night!

Ossian.

EXERCISES.

Analysis.

1. How many *sentences* in the above extract?
2. Classify the *first* sentence as to *form*[1] and *use*[2].
3. Give its *subject-nominative*.
4. Give its *predicate-adjective* (or *attribute*).
5. Give its *predicate-verb* (or *copula*).
6. Name the *independent* phrase.
7. What is the *base* or *chief* part of this phrase?
8. By *what* is the *base* modified?
9. What *gender* is "*daughter*"? 10. What *person*?
11. Give the corresponding *masculine* of "*daughter.*"
12. Classify the *second* sentence as to *form* and *use*.
13. Give its *entire subject;* 14. its *entire predicate*.
15. Give the *modifiers* of the subject. 16. Of the *predicate-verb*.
17. Give the *adjective* in predication.
18. To *what* does this *adjective* relate?
19. What *kind* of sentence is the *third*, as to *form* and *use*?
20. Give its *simple subject;* 21. its *entire predicate*.
22. Give its *simple predicate* (or *verb*).
23. What does "*forth*" modify?
24. Give the *simple subject* of the *fourth* sentence.
25. Give the *simple predicate*.
26. Give the *simple* (or *unmodified*) *object*.
27. For what does "*thy*" stand? 28. Give the gender of "*thy*."
29. What does "*in the east*" modify?
30. Classify the *fifth* sentence as to *form* and *use*.
31. Write a sentence and draw a line under its *principal elements* (or *parts*).
32. Is the phrase "*in thy presence*," adjective or *adverbial* in office?
33. What *independent* words accompany this sentence?
34. Give the *entire predicate* of the *sixth* sentence.
35. Give its *predicate-verb;* 36. its *object*.
37. By what is the *object* modified?

---

[1] Simple, complex, or compound.
[2] Declarative, interrogative, imperative, or exclamatory.

38. What *noun* does "*their*" represent?
39. Select a *compound* word.
40. Classify the *last sentence* of the extract as to *form* and *use*.
41. What *independent* phrase does it contain?
42. Give the *subject-nominative* of this sentence.
43. Give its *predicate-verb*.
44. What part of speech is "*like*"?
45. Of what is "*thee*" the *object?*
46. What does "*in heaven*" modify?
47. What is meant by the phrase, "*light of the silent night*"?
48. Define *Orthography*. 49. *Etymology*. 50. *Syntax*.

Synthesis.

Write in separate sentences and indicate by the *underscore*, the following:

1. A *polysyllabic* word.
2. A *compound* word *modified*.
3. A word having a *prefix*.
4. A word having a *suffix*.
5. A plural noun formed by changing *f*, or *fe*, into *ves*.
6. A plural noun ending in *ies*.
7. A noun whose plural is formed *irregularly*.
8. A word in which *y* final is changed to *i* in the *derivative* word.
9. A word in which *y* final is unchanged in the *derivative* word.
10. A word illustrating the *penultimate* accent.
11. A word illustrating the *antepenultimate* accent.
12. The plural of *man-servant*. 13. Of *knight-templar*.
14. The plural of *a*. 15. Of *5*.

False Syntax.

1. A lion is bold.
2. Richard Third was bad king.
3. There was no doubt of its being them.
4. The four sisters were tenderly attached to each other.
5. There are less apples now than this morning.

EXERCISES.

6. "Interesting" is accented on the former syllable.
7. Rebecca took goodly raiment and put them on Jacob.
8. What are the news? Are they good?
9. Night, sable goddess, from his ebon throne.
10. There was a chance of him recovering his money.

EXERCISE VI.

1. No mate, no comrade, Lucy knew;
2. She dwelt on a wild moor;
3. The sweetest thing that ever grew,
4. Beside a cottage door.

5. You yet may spy the lamb at play,
6. The hare upon the green;
7. But the sweet face of Lucy Gray
8. Will never more be seen.

Wordsworth.

Analysis.

1. How many *sentences* in the above stanzas?
2. Classify the first sentence as to *form* (simple, complex, or compound).
3. State the *number of clauses* in this sentence.
4. Give its *co-ordinate* propositions.
5. Give its *subordinate* proposition.
6. Which proposition has a *compound* object?
7. Select a noun in the *nominative* case from the first stanza.
8. Select an *adjective*. 9. A *transitive* verb.
10. A *relative* pronoun. 11. A *preposition*.
12. An *adverb*. 13. An *adverbial* phrase.
14. An adjective in the *superlative* degree.

EXERCISES.

15. Give the gender of "*mate.*" 16. Of "*thing.*"
17. Classify the *second* sentence as to *form.*
18. Give its *first* proposition.
19. Give the *predicate-verb* of this proposition; 20. the *object.*
21. What does "*yet*" modify?
22. What does "*at play*" modify?
23. What does "*upon the green*" modify?
24. Give the *co-ordinate* connective of this sentence.
25. What does "*sweet*" modify?
26. What does "*of Lucy Gray*" modify?
27. Give the *part of speech* of "*never.*"
28. To what does it belong?
29. What *part of speech* is "*more*"?
30. To what does it belong?
31. Give the *gender* of "*lamb.*"
32. In what *mood* is "*may spy*"?
33. Give the *gender* of "*hare.*"
34. In what tense is "*may spy*"? 35. Give its object.
36. Give the *case* of "*face.*"
37. In what *mood* is the verb in the eighth line?
38. In what *tense?* 39. Give its *voice.*
40. Has this verb an *object?*
41. Give the four principal parts of "*see.*"
42. What word *usually* a noun is used as an *adjective* in the first stanza?
43. What word *usually* an adjective is used as a *noun* in the second stanza?
44. Change the fifth line to the *corresponding* interrogative proposition.
45. Select a word containing a *silent* vowel.
46. Select a word having a *silent* consonant.
47. Select an adjective used in two of its degrees of comparison.
48. Define a *phrase.* 49. A *clause.* 50. A *compound* sentence.

Synthesis.

Write in separate sentences and indicate by the *underscore*, the following:

1. A noun of the *masculine* gender.

2. A noun of the *feminine* gender.
3. A noun of the *neuter* gender.
4. A noun of the *common* gender.
5. *If* in the *plural* number.
6. *Axis* in the *plural* number.
7. *Bandit* in the objective plural.
8. A noun used in the plural number *only*.
9. A noun having the same form for either number.
10. *Beau* in the *possessive* plural.
11. *Cherub* in *nominative* plural.
12. Write a sentence having a *compound*[1] subject.
13. A *compound*[2] predicate. 14. A *compound*[3] object.
15. Write a sentence having the *subject*, the *predicate*, and the *object*, all compound.

[1] Two or more subject-nominatives to the *same* verb.
[2] Two or more predicate-verbs relating to the *same* subject.
[3] Two or more substantives as the object of the *same* verb.

False Syntax.

1. I would not desire to be him.
2. Milton is more sublime than any of the poets.
3. Henry is the tallest of the two.
4. He is an old, respectable man.
5. Have you any new children's shoes?
6. This was the most unkindest cut of all.
7. This was the more noble Roman of them all.
8. This is the pet lamb whom all admire.
9. The committee have performed its task.
10. He wore a knight's templars sword.

EXERCISE VII.

In slumbers of midnight the sailor-boy lay;
His hammock swung loose at the sport of the wind;
But watch-worn and weary, his cares flew away;
And visions of happiness danced o'er his mind.
           - *Dimond.*

Analysis.

1. Is the above sentence *simple, complex,* or *compound?*
2. Of how many *clauses* is it composed?
3. Of how many *propositions?*
4. Is a clause *always* a *proposition?*
5. May a *simple* sentence ever contain a clause?
6. What *propositions* does *but* connect?
7. Give the *simple subject* of the *first* proposition.
8. Give the *predicate-verb.*
9. By what is the *subject* modified?
10. By what is the *predicate* modified?
11. What does "*of midnight*" modify?
12. What is the *complete subject* of the second proposition?
13. Give its *complete predicate.*
14. Give its *simple subject.*
15. Give its *simple predicate.*
16. By what is "*hammock*" modified?
17. By what is "*swung*" modified?
18. What does "*of the wind*" modify?
19. To what do "*watch-worn*" and "*weary*" relate?
20. What is the *antecedent* of "*his*"?
21. Give the *part of speech* of "*in.*"
22. Of "*swung.*" 23. Of "*loose.*" 24. Of "*at.*"

25. Of "*sport.*" 26. Of "*weary.*" 27. Of "*away.*"
28. Of "*visions.*" 29. Of "*happiness.*" 30. Of "*danced.*"
31. Of "*o'er.*" 32. Of "*his.*" 33. Of "*mind.*"
34. Select a *primitive* word. 35. A *derivative* word.
36. Select a *compound* word.
37. Write the *possessive* of "*slumbers.*" 38. Of "*sailor-boy.*"
39. What *mood* is used throughout the Exercise?
40. What *tense*?
41. Is "*w*" a *vowel*, or a *consonant*, in "*weary*"?
42. Is "*y*" a *vowel*, or a *consonant*, in "*weary*"?
43. Is "*ea*" a *proper*, or an *improper* diphthong?
44. Change the verb of the last line to the *progressive* form, same tense.
45. What word has two *silent* letters?
46. Give the *principal* parts of a *verb* in *first* line.
47. Of the *verb* in the *third* line.
48. Define a *collective* noun. 49. An *abstract* noun.
50. Define a *verbal* or *participial* noun.

Synthesis.

Combine into appropriate sentences the following elements, and *underscore* each element:

1. A *prepositional* phrase (one introduced by a preposition).
2. A *participial* phrase (one introduced by a participle).
3. An *infinitive* phrase (one introduced by an infinitive verb), unmodified, or otherwise.
4. A *simple* phrase. 5. A *complex* phrase.
6. A *compound* phrase.
7. A phrase used *adjectively.*
8. A phrase used *adverbially.*
9. A phrase used *substantively.*
10. A phrase used *independently* (not *grammatically* connected).
11. A phrase expressing *time;* 12. *manner;* 13. *place.*
14. An *adjective* phrase and an *adverbial* phrase.
15. A phrase with a preposition *understood.*

False Syntax.

1. This State exports more cotton than all the states.
2. That large oak is the taller of the three.
3. He obtained a living by that means.
4. That moon was the roundest of any.
5. We took a pleasant and new way.
6. Which do you prefer most, apples or oranges?
7. He is an exceeding good boy.
8. Velvet feels smoothly.
9. The good's must be returned to-morrow.
10. Everything is judged by it's use.

EXERCISE VIII

1. It was noontide. The sun was very hot. An old
2. gentlewoman sat spinning in a little arbor
3. at the door. She was blind; and her grand-
4. daughter was reading the Bible to her. The
5. old lady had just left her work, to attend to the
6. story of Ruth. — *Chas. Lamb.*

Analysis.

1. Give the *number of sentences* in the above extract.
2. Give the *number of clauses*.
3. Give the *number of propositions*.
4. Are any of the sentences other than *declarative?*
5. Are any of them other than *simple?*
6. Select the sentence having *two propositions*.
7. Are these propositions *independent*, or *dependent?*
8. If *independent*, how would you classify the sentence as to *form?*
9–20. Write all the *subject-nominatives* of the extract and after each, its *predicate-verb*.

21-25. Write all the *descriptive* (or *qualifying*) *adjectives* and give the noun or pronoun to which each relates.
26-27. Select the *adverbs* and tell what each modifies.
28. Select a *predicate-nominative*.
29. Select an *incomparable* adjective.
30. Give the *nominative* form of the pronoun that supplies three cases.
31. Name the *cases* thus represented.
32. Compare "*little*"; 33. "*old*."
34. Select a *common* noun *feminine* gender.
35. Select a *proper* noun *feminine* gender.
36. Select a *proper* noun *neuter* gender.
37. What does "*in a little arbor*" modify?
38. What does "*at the door*" modify?
39. Select an *adjective phrase*.
40. Select an *adverbial phrase*.
41. Select an *infinitive phrase* (verb in the infinitive mood).
42. What does *this phrase* modify?
43. Select a verb in the *past* tense.
44. Select a verb in the *progressive* form.
45. What part of speech is "*spinning*"?
46. To what does it belong?
47. Why should "*Bible*" begin with a capital letter?
48. Define a *monosyllable;* 49. *dissyllable;* 50. *trisyllable*

Synthesis.

1. Write a complex sentence having an *adjective* clause.
2. One having an *adverbial* clause.
3. One with a *noun-clause* in the *nominative* case.

Write in separate sentences and *underscore* the following:

4. The plural of *madame*. 5. Of *memorandum*.
6. Of *mouse-trap*.
7. A *collective* noun in the plural—*shown by the verb*.
8. Shown by a *pronoun* referring to the collective noun.
9. A *collective* noun of the *singular, neuter*, as shown by the verb.
10. A *masculine* noun by *personification*.
11. A *feminine* noun by *personification*,
12. The corresponding opposite gender of *buck*.
13. Of *Earl*. 14. Of *stag*. 15. Of *witch*.

False Syntax.

1. The nice apples are on the fartherest limb.
2. The opinion was more universal than was at first believed.
3. Of two evils, choose the least.
4. Hand me them books.
5. Run quick into the house.
6. The trader bought twenty heads of cattle.
7. John, he has broke a window.
8. The jury who were out all night has just returned a verdict.
9. The moon kept on his course.
10. In no case are writers so apt to err as in the word *only*.

MACAULAY.

EXERCISE IX.

1. Woodman, spare that tree!
2. Touch not a single bough!
3. In youth it sheltered me,
4. And I'll protect it now.
5. 'Twas my forefather's hand
6. That placed it near his cot;
7. Then, woodman, let it stand,
8. Thy axe shall harm it not.

Geo. P. Morris.

Analysis.

1. How many *sentences* in the above stanza?
2. Classify the first sentence as to *form* and *use*.
3. Give its *subject*; 4. its *predicate-verb*.
5. Give its *object*.
6. What *independent* word has this sentence?

7. What part of speech is "*that*"? 8. Give its *plural.*
9. Classify the first *declarative* sentence as *complex*, or *compound*.
10. Give its *connective.*
11. What does "*in youth*" modify?
12. Give the *gender* of "*youth*" as here used.
13. Classify the last sentence as to *form.*
14. Classify the same as to *use.*
15. What clause is not *declarative* in this sentence?
16. Should this fact be stated in connection with the *classification ?*
17. Give the *subordinate* clause of this sentence.
18. What does this *clause* modify?
19. What connects it to the *preceding* clause?
20. What *part of speech* is this *connective ?*
21. Select from the stanza a pronoun, third person, nominative case.
22. Select a *predicate-nominative.*
23. An *adverb of time.* 24. Of *negation.*
25. A verb in the *imperative* mood.
26. A verb in the *indicative* mood *future* tense.
27. Give the part of speech of "*single.*"
28. Of "*then.*" 29. Of "*stand.*"
30. Give the antecedent of "*it,*" third line. 31. Of "*his.*"
32. In what case is "*cot ?*"
33. Give the rule for its *case,*
34. Give the *possessive singular* of "*it.*"
35. Give the *possessive plural* of "*it.*"
36. Give the *possessive plural* of "*axe.*"
37. What pronoun has the same form in *two cases ?*
38. Give the *principal parts* of "*let.*"
39. Of "*stand.*" 40. Of "*harm.*"
41. Select an *auxiliary* verb.
42. What *person* is "*woodman*"?
43. Give its *plural possessive.*
44. Change the last line to the *corresponding interrogative* proposition.
45. Change the same to the *corresponding passive* proposition.
46. What is the name of the character "*'*" in "*I'll*"?
47. What does this character *signify* when thus used?
48. Define a *letter;* 49. a *vowel;* 50. a *consonant.*

EXERCISES. 49

Synthesis.

Re-write the following sentences and supply the *proper* pronoun in the blank spaces:
1. Grim-visaged war hath smoothed —— angry front.
2. White-winged peace offers —— olive branch.
3. The lion meets —— foe boldly.
4. The nightingale sings —— evening song.
5. The bee builds —— cells now as at first.
6. The infant was lying in —— cradle.
7. The horse eats —— oats with satisfaction.
8. The goose stretches out —— neck.
9. There march a train with baskets on —— heads.
10. Mankind directed —— first care to the useful.
11. The jury could not agree in —— opinions.
12. The council was a unit in —— decision.
13. The multitude pursue pleasure as —— only delight.
14. The committee of ladies and gentlemen expressed (itself? or themselves?) as a unit.
15. The ship, with —— snowy sails, soon hove in sight.

False Syntax.

1. The sixteen first soldiers marched by twos.
2. The class whom we heard acquitted itself finely.
3. Each of the combatants wore their visors up.
4. Who who is honest will deny the fact?
5. The lion is an animal who meets his foe boldly.
6. The chestnuts are our'n.
7. He gave it to the Captain's of the Baltic's wife.
8. Xerxes army was large.
9. He from my childhood I have known.
10. The lord cannot refuse to admit the heir of his tenant upon his death; nor can he remove his present tenant as long as he lives.

BLACKSTONE.

EXERCISE X.

Hands of angels hidden from mortal eyes shifted the scenery of the heavens; the glories of night dissolved into the glories of the dawn. The blue sky now turned more softly gray; the great watch-stars shut up their holy eyes. The east began to kindle, and soon the great celestial concave was filled with the inflowing tides of the morning light.

Everett.

Analysis.

1. State the number of *sentences* in the above extract.
2. Classify the *first* sentence as to *form* and *use*.
3. Give the *entire subject* of the *first* member.
4. Give its *entire predicate;* 5. its *subject-nominative*.
6. Give its *predicate-verb*. 7. Give its *simple* object.
8. Select from this member an *adjective* phrase, *participial in form.*
9. Select an *adjective* phrase, *prepositional in form.*
10. Select an *adverbial* phrase.
11. Give the *entire subject* of the *second* member.
12. Give its *entire predicate*.
13. What *complex* phrase modifies the *predicate-verb*?
14. Classify the *second* sentence as *complex,* or *compound.*
15. What *adjectives* are found in its *first* member?
16. What ones are found in its *second* member?
17. Select from this sentence an *adverb of time,*
18. And one of *degree.*
19. What is the *antecedent* of "*their*"?
20. Classify the last sentence as *complex,* or *compound.*
21-24. Give the *subject-nominative* and *predicate-verb* of each of its propositions.

EXERCISES.

25. In what *mood* are all the verbs of the extract?
26. In what *tense?*
27. Which verbs are *transitive active?*
28. Which one is *transitive passive?*
29. Select the *infinitive verb.*
30. Is this infinitive, *adverbial,* or *substantive* in office?
31. Select an *incomparable* adjective.
32. Is "*inflowing*" a participial (or verbal) adjective?
33. Give the principal parts of "*began.*"
34. In what degree of comparison is "*gray*"?
35. What *part of speech* is "*softly*"?
36. In what *degree* is "*softly*"?
37. Select a *primitive* word.
38. A *derivative* word, and
39. A *compound* word.
40. Give the rule for doubling the "*d*" in "*hidden.*"
41. What gender is "*angels*"?
42. What *word* connects the last two *propositions?*
43. Does this conjunction ever connect *other* than *co-ordinate* elements?
44. Classify "*y*" in "*holy.*"
45. Classify "*w*" in "*was.*"
46. What *silent* letters occur in "*light*"?
47. When is a letter said to be *silent?*
48. Give the *modifiers* (or *adjuncts*) of "*tides.*"
49. Define a *primitive* word.
50. Define a *compound* word.

Synthesis.

1. Write a *complex interrogative* sentence.
2. Write a *complex imperative* sentence.
4. Write in a sentence the plural of *goose* (iron for pressing).
5. The plural of *ellipsis.*
6. Of *Mr.* 7. Of the pronoun *I.*
8. Of *Miss Smith.* 9. Of *Mr. Brown.*
10. The plural *form* of a *collective* noun.

11. Write in a sentence the corresponding opposite gender of *hero*.
12. Of *he-goat* in the nominative plural.
13. Of *friar* in the objective plural.
14. Of *Sir* in the *nominative independent*.
15. Write a sentence containing six different parts of speech.

False Syntax.

1. Virtue and vice are opposite qualities; this ennobles the mind, that debases it.
2. We saw the prisoners and arms which were captured.
3. Neither the merchant nor the lawyer made themselves rich.
4. This is the same friend who was here. .
5. Every man and every boy received their wages.
6. The parent's care for her children is a divine instinct.
7. John told his father that his brother had come.
8. It was he, not William's fault.
9. The novel is one of Scott.
10. Let a gallows be erected of fifty cubits high. BIBLE.

EXERCISE XI.

The breaking waves dashed high on a stern and rock-
 bound coast,
And the woods against a stormy sky their giant branches
 tossed,
And the heavy night hung dark the hills and waters o'er,
When a band of exiles moored their bark on the wild
 New England shore.

Mrs. Hemans.

Analysis.

1. What kind of *sentence* is the above as to *form*?
2. Of how many *clauses* is it composed?
3. Give the *first* and the *last* word of the *dependent* clause.
4. What does this *clause* modify?
5. Give the *connective*.
6. What *other* office does this *connective* perform?

7-11. Write all the *prepositional* phrases and state what each modifies.

Write each of the following words and describe it as *subject-nominative, predicate-verb, object, adjective modifier*, as the case may be, of the word or words, to which it is syntactically related, *giving such word or words:*

12. "*Breaking*"; 13. "*waves*"; 14. "*dashed*"; 15. "*high*";
16. "*stern*"; 17. "*coast*"; 18. "*their*"; 19. "*giant*";
20. "*branches*"; 21. "*tossed*"; 22. "*heavy*"; 23. "*night*";
24. "*hung*"; 25. "*dark*"; 26. "*hills*"; 27. "*waters*";
28. "*band*"; 29. "*exiles*"; 30. "*bark*"; 31. "*wild*";
32. "*New England*"; 33. "*shore.*"

34. Give the antecedent of "*their*," *second* clause.
35. Give the gender of "*their*," *last* clause.
36. Select a *collective* noun. 37. Give its *gender*.
38. Give the *number* of "*moored*."
39. In what *mood* are all the verbs?
40. In what *tense*?
41. Select the *proper* adjective.
42. Select a *compound* adjective.
43. Select a *verbal* (or *participial*) adjective.
44. Can this adjective be *compared* with propriety?
45. Mention a part of speech *not found* in the above stanza.
46. Give the rule for capitalizing "*New England.*"
47. What sound has "*e*" in "*England*"?
48. Define a *pronoun*.
49. Define a *personal* pronoun.
50. Define a *relative* pronoun.

EXERCISES.

Synthesis.

Write in separate sentences, and *underscore*, the following:
1. Your own name in the *possessive* case.
2. A noun in the *nominative case* by *direct address*.
3. By *exclamation*. 4. By *pleonasm*.
5. A noun in the *nominative-absolute before* a participle.
6. *Nominative absolute after* a participle.
7. *After* an *infinitive*.
8. A noun used as a *predicate-nominative*.
9. *Sheep* in the *possessive plural*.
10. *Conscience* in the *possessive singular*.
11. *Knight-errant* in the *possessive plural*.
12. The corresponding opposite gender of *Czar*.
13. The possessive plural of the opposite gender of *cock-robin*.
14. *Richard the Third*, in the possessive singular.
15. A compound personal pronoun in *apposition*.

False Syntax.

1. The court has reserved their judgment.
2. You and your companions may go to their sports.
3. The cat or the dog must have taken their share.
4. They are wolves in sheep's clothing.
5. John, Henry and William's nose resembled one another.
6. John's uncle's brother's farm lies in the valley.
7. She that is studious, commend heartily.
8. Who do you think was with me last evening?
9. A variety of pleasing objects charm the eye.
10. They seem to have been tyro's. SWIFT.

EXERCISE XII.

Captain John Hull was the mint-master of Massachusetts, and coined all the money that was used there. This was a new line of business; for, in the earlier days of the colony, the current coinage consisted of gold and silver money of England, Portugal, and Spain. These coins being scarce, the people were often forced to barter their commodities instead of selling them.

Nathaniel Hawthorne.

Analysis.

1. How many *sentences* in the above selection?
2. Is the first one *complex*, or *compound*?
3. Give the *subject-nominative* of the *first* clause.
4. Give the *entire predicate*.
5–6. Give the *subject-nominative* and *predicate-verb* of the *second* clause.
7. Is the second sentence *complex*, or *compound?*
8–11. Give the *simple subject* and *predicate* of each proposition.
12. Classify the last sentence as *simple* or *compound*.
13. Give its *entire subject*. 14. Give its *entire predicate*.
15. Give its *subject-nominative*. 16. Give its *predicate-verb*.
17. What *independent* phrase in the extract?
18. Give its *base*, or *chief* word.
19. Select a *present* participle used *adjectively*.
20. Select a *present* participle used *substantively* (*like a noun*).
21. Select an *adjective* phrase. 22. An *adverbial* phrase.
23. A *complex* phrase. 24. A *prepositional* phrase.
25. A *predicate-nominative*. 26. Give its modifiers.
27. What word connects the two *clauses* of the *second* sentence?
28. What *part of speech* is this connective?

EXERCISES.

29. Is it *co-ordinate*, or *subordinate*?
30. What part of speech is "*selling*," as here used?
31. Has this word *case*?
32. By what rule would you parse "*selling*"?
33. What is the *subsequent* term of relation of the *preposition* preceding?
34. Name this *preposition*?
35. Select an *infinitive verb*.
36. What does it modify?
37. Select a noun used *absolutely* (or *independently*).
38. What part of speech is "*scarce*"?
39. To what does it *relate*?
40. Select a verb in the *passive voice*.
41. Select an *adverb* of *place*.
42. Select an adjective in the *comparative* degree.
43. Give the antecedent of "*their*."
44. For what does "*them*" stand?
45. Give the plural possessive of "*money*."
46. In what *mood* are all the verbs?
47. In what *tense*?
48. Define an *interrogative* pronoun.
49. Define "*gender*." 50. Define a *triphthong*.

Synthesis.

1. Write a sentence containing a *verbal* (or *participial*) adjective.
2. Write a declarative sentence in which the subject comes after the verb.
3. Write a sentence having an *appositive* phrase.
4. Write a sentence containing the possessive plural of *mousetrap*. 5. Of *spoonful*.
6. Of *brother-in-law*. 7. Of *hanger-on*.
8. Of *woman-servant*. 9. Of *dor-mouse*.
10. Write in a sentence the corresponding opposite gender of *abbot*. 11. Of *testator*.
12. Of *roe*. 13. Of *duke*.
14. Write a sentence containing three *personal* pronouns.
15. Compose a sentence having *all* the parts of speech.

False Syntax.

1. Each day and each hour bring contrary blessings.
2. I, you, and James were invited.
3. You, James, and I broke the buggy.
4. Ferdinand's and Isabella's united aid was asked by Columbus.
5. Let thou and I the battle try.
6. Who are you going to vote for?
7. The dead warrior looked fiercely.
8. Was it me that you saw?
9. Such phenomena is very strange.
10. Please to read slow and plain.

EXERCISE XIII.

1. Beauty is an all-prevailing presence. It unfolds in
2. the numberless flowers of the spring. It waves in the
3. branches of the trees and the green blades of grass. It
4. haunts the depths of the earth and sea, and gleams out in
5. the hue of the shell and precious stone. The universe is its
6. temple; and those men who are alive to it, cannot lift up
7. their eyes without feeling themselves encompassed with it
8. on every side.

Channing.

Analysis.

1-8. Give the *simple subject* and *predicate* of each of the first four propositions.

9-12. Write all the *descriptive* (or *qualifying*) adjectives of these propositions.

13. Draw a line under those *not comparable*.
14. Select from the Exercise a *predicate nominative.*

EXERCISES.

15. An *adverbial* phrase. 16. An *adjective* phrase.
17. A *prepositional* phrase. 18. A *simple* phrase.
19. A *complex* phrase.
20. What subject has a *compound* predicate?
21. In what *mood* are the verbs of this predicate?
22. Classify the *last sentence* of the Exercise.
23. Name its *co-ordinate* propositions.
24. What word *connects* them?
25. Name the *subordinate* clause of this sentence.
26. Is this clause *adjective,* or *adverbial* in office?
27. On what does it depend?
28. Name the *connecting* word of this clause?
29. Select from the sentence a *plural definitive* adjective.
30. Give its *singular* form.
31. Give the part of speech of "*who.*"
32. Of "*alive.*" 33. Of "*up.*" 34. Of "*without.*"
35. Of "*feeling.*" 36. Of "*encompassed.*" 37. Of "*with.*"
38. What *tense* is used throughout the Exercise?
39. Name the *transitive* verbs. 40. Decline "*who*"; 41. "*men.*"
42. Give the antecedent of "*it,*" sixth line.
43. Of "*their,*" in the same line.
44. Of "*themselves,*" in the seventh line.
45. Can *themselves* properly be used in the *nominative* case?
46. Select a verb in the *potential* mood.
47. Give the two terms of relation of "*without.*"
48. Define *person.* 49. *Number.* 50. *Case.*

Synthesis.

Write in separate sentences the possessive plural of the following words:

1. The pronoun *I.*
2. *Court-martial.*
3. *Wagon-load.*
4. *Piano-forte.*
5. *Jack-a-lantern.*
6. *Knight-templar.*
7. *Ox.*
8. *Child.*
9. *Miss.*
10. *Attorney-general.*
11. *Summons.*
12. *Man-of-war.*
13. *Man-of-war's-man.*
14. *Alumnus.*
15. Write a sentence having a *noun-clause* in the objective case.

False Syntax.

1. It is very painful to have a tooth pulled.
2. I rode the commander's-in-chief's horse.
3. There was no doubt of him being promoted.
4. His sister-in-laws were present.
5. All went except he.
6. Between you and I, he is a little crazy.
7. How can we tell who to trust.
8. He and I was working in the same field.
9. Twenty head of cattle was passing.
10. She works well and neat.

EXERCISE XIV.

1. I saw from the beach when the morning was shining,
2. A bark o'er the waters move gloriously on;
3. I came when the sun o'er that beach was declining—
4. The bark was still there but the waters were gone.
Moore.

5. Not a drum was heard, not a funeral note,
6. As his corse to the rampart we hurried;
7. Not a soldier discharged his farewell shot,
8. O'er the grave where our hero was buried.
Wolf.

Analysis.

1. How many *sentences* in both stanzas?
2. Classify the first as *complex* or *compound*.
3. Give the *reason* for your classification.
4–9. Give the *simple subject* and *predicate* of three of the *principal* propositions of the first stanza.

10–13. Give the same of its *subordinate* propositions.
14. Give the *co-ordinate* connective.
15. Give the *subordinate* connectives.
16. What *part of speech* are these subordinate connectives?
17–19. Name the *adverbial* phrases and state what each modifies.
20. Do these phrases express *time*, *place*, *degree*, or *manner?*
21. Answer the same question with reference to the *subordinate* clauses.
22. Select the *transitive* verb in this sentence.
23. What part of speech is "*on*"?
24. Give its syntactical office.
25. Select an *adverb of time*.
26. Select an *adverb of place*.
27. Select an *adverb of manner*.
28. Is "*were gone*" a *transitive* verb? 29. Has it *voice?*
30. What *kind of sentence* as to *form* is the second stanza?
31. Of how many *propositions* is it composed?
32. Name the *co-ordinate* propositions.
33. Name the *subordinate* propositions.
34. What does the *first* one modify? 35. Give its *connective*.
36. What does the *last* clause modify?
37. Is it *adjective*, or *adverbial* in office?
38. Give its *connective*.
39. What *part of speech* is this *connective?*
40. What *part of speech* is the first "*not*," line 5?
41. What does it *modify?*
42. What does "*to the rampart*" modify?
43. Give the *syntax* of the second "*not*."
44. Give the possessive plural of "*hero*."
45. Give its *corresponding feminine*.
46. What *mood* have all the verbs of the last stanza?
47. What *tense* is used throughout the same?
48. Define the *masculine* gender.
49. Define an *improper* diphthong.
50. Into what *general* classes are letters divided?

Synthesis.

1. Write a sentence expressing by the possessive case *joint* ownership of a store by Brown and Smith.
2. Express in a sentence by the possessive case *separate* ownership by Brown and Smith.
3. Write a sentence with a noun in the *possessive* case by apposition.
4. With a noun used as the object of an infinitive verb.
5. With a noun used as the object of a participle.
6. With a pronoun used as the object of a preposition understood.
7. With a predicate-nominative after some verb *other* than *be* or *become*.
8. With a predicate-nominative after a passive verb (verb in passive voice).
9. Compose a sentence containing a *pronominal* adjective.
10. A *numeral* adjective.
11. A *compound* adjective.
12. A *definitive* (limiting) adjective.
13. A *proper* adjective modifying a predicate-nominative.
14. An *ordinal* numeral adjective.
15. A *participial* adjective modified.

False Syntax.

1. Many a flower must waste their sweetness.
2. That fine orator and statesman will deliver their lecture to-night.
3. There was a certain householder which planted a vineyard.
4. The book is at Smith's and Brown's store.
5. I can run as fast as him.
6. You will repent you of your foolish choice.
7. Between the three brothers, no contention had ever occurred.
8. It could not be them whom you saw.
9. Has the cows been fed?
10. My cause and thine is one. DRYDEN.

EXERCISE XV.

Marley was dead to begin with. There was no doubt about that. The register of his burial was signed by the clergyman, the clerk, the undertaker, and the chief mourner. Scrooge signed it; and Scrooge's name was good upon 'Change' for anything he chose to put his hand to. Old Marley was as dead as a door-nail. *Dickens.*

Analysis.

1. How many *simple* sentences in the extract?
2. Which sentence is *compound?*
3. Which one is *complex?*
4. Give the *co-ordinate* propositions.
5. Select a clause used *adjectively.*
6. Select one used *adverbially.*
7. What does the *adverbial* clause modify?
8. What connects it to the *principal* clause?
9. What does the *adjective* clause modify?
10. What connects it to the *principal* clause?
11. What connects the *co-ordinate* propositions?
12. Give the *construction* of "*to begin with.*"
13. Give the syntax of "*with.*"

14–29. Write the *subject-nominative*, and immediately thereafter, the *predicate-verb* of each proposition of the Exercise.

30. Change "Scrooge signed it" to the corresponding *passive* form.
31. What part of speech is "*dead*"?
32. What is the rule for parsing the *infinitive verb* in the first sentence?
33. What part of speech is "*there*"?
34. Give the *reason* for your answer to the above question.

EXERCISES. 63

35. Give the rule for parsing "*there.*"
36. What pronoun is *understood* in one of the propositions?
37. What *ellipsis* occurs in another proposition?
38. Select a *preposition* having a *compound* object.
39. What does the *phrase* modify?
40. Select a noun in the *possessive* case.
41. Parse the *last* word in the *fourth* sentence.
42. Give the rule for parsing "*to put.*"
43. What *part of speech* is the *first* "*as*" in the *last* sentence?
44. The second "*as*"?
45. Select an *adverbial* phrase of *place*.
46. Select a *definitive* (or *limiting*) adjective.
47. What does "*about that*" modify?
48. What does "*that*" stand for, or represent?
49. Define a *root*. 50. Define a *prefix*.

Synthesis.

1. Write a sentence containing an adjective and a prepositional phrase limiting the subject.
2. Add to the above an adverb and an adverbial phrase.
3. Write a sentence having the subject modified by three adjectives.
4. One containing two auxiliary verbs.
5. A sentence having an adjective modified by an adverb.
6. Write a sentence containing two objective words, two adverbs, and two articles.

Write in separate sentences and *underscore* the following:

7. A cardinal numeral adjective.
8. A multiplicative numeral adjective.
9. An adjective in the comparative degree.
10. An adjective in the superlative degree.
11. An incomparable adjective.
12. The adjectives *evil* and *good* in the superlative degree.
13. The adjectives *little* and *many* in the comparative degree.
14. The adjectives *fore* and *near* in the superlative degree.
15. The adjectives *old* and *late* in the comparative degree.

False Syntax.

1. Would you just as leave go?
2. Go where ox-lips and the nodding violet grows.
3. The lady was the first who called.
4. We cannot allow of such things.
5. The money was divided among the two.
6. The Senate have adjourned.
7. *Horses* are a common noun.
8. Many a captain with all the crew have been lost at sea.
9. Our heavy task is not near done.
10. I never did repent of doing good, nor shall not now.

SHAKESPEARE.

EXERCISE XVI.

Full many a gem of purest ray serene,
    The dark unfathomed caves of ocean bear;
Full many a flower is born to blush unseen,
    And waste its sweetness on the desert air.

Some village Hampden, that, with dauntless breast,
    The little tyrant of his field withstood—
Some mute, inglorious Milton, here may rest;
    Some Cromwell, guiltless of his country's blood.

Gray's Elegy.

Analysis.

1. Classify the *first sentence* of the extract as to *form*.
2. How many *propositions* does it contain?
3. Give the *entire subject* of the first proposition.
4. Give its *entire predicate*. 5. Give its *subject-nominative*.
6. Give its *predicate-verb*.

7-10. Answer the *last four* directions with reference to the *second* proposition.

State whether the following elements are *adjective* or *adverbial* in office, and on what each depends :

11. "*Full*"; 12. "*many a*"; 13. "*of purest ray serene*";
14. "*serene*"; 15. "*dark*"; 16. "*of ocean*"; 17. "*to blush*";
18. "*unseen*"; 19. "*its*"; 20. "*on the desert air.*"

21. In what *case* is "*gem*"?
22. Give the antecedent of "*its.*"
23. Select a verb in the *potential* mood.
24. Give the tense of "*bear.*" 25. Give its *principal parts.*
26. Give the *mood* of "*is born.*" 27. Is it *transitive*?
28. Classify the second stanza as a *complex*, or a *compound* sentence.
29. Mention its *co-ordinate* propositions.
30. Give its *subordinate* clause.
31. Is this clause *adjective*, or *adverbial* in office?
32. What connects it to the *principal* clause?
33. Of which clause is this *connective* a part?
34. What part of speech is "*village*"?
35. What does "*with dauntless breast*" modify?
36. What *phrase* modifier has "*tyrant*"?
37. Is "*of his country's blood*" *adjective*, or *adverbial* in office?
38. Write the *plural possessive* of "*country.*"
39. Select from the stanzas an adjective in the *superlative* degree.
40. Select an adjective *not commonly compared.*
41. Give the *mood* of "*may rest.*"
42. Has this verb an *object*?
43. Why does "*Hampden*" begin with a capital?
44. Is "*Milton*" as here used a *common* or *proper* noun?
45. Give the *reason* for your answer.
46. What *ellipsis* must be supplied in the last stanza, if *any*?
47. In what *case* is "*tyrant*"?
48. Define a *noun.* 49. Define a *common* noun.
50. Define a *proper* noun.

EXERCISES.

Synthesis.

1. Write a sentence with a predicate adjective modified by a phrase.
2. A sentence with an adjective taken abstractly (or absolutely) after a *subject* infinitive.
3. An adjective taken abstractly or absolutely after a participle.
4. An adjective used for an adverb, by poetic license.
5. An adjective used as a noun.
6. An adjective (not in predicate) following its noun.
7. An adjective relating to a pronoun in the objective case.
8. An adjective belonging to a participial noun.
9. Write a sentence using *which* as an adjective.
10. Compose a sentence using the same personal pronoun in two different cases.
11. Write a simple sentence containing a personal pronoun agreeing with its antecedent in the third, masculine, singular.
12. In the third, feminine, singular.
13. In the third, neuter, singular.
14. In the third, common, plural.
15. Write a complex sentence with two dependent clauses.

False Syntax.

1. The jury said it must have its dinner.
2. Winter comes shaking its shaggy beard.
3. Russia and Turkey's armies fought many battles.
4. Satan, than who, none higher sat.
5. Whom do men say I am?
6. The *Pleasures of Hope* were read to the company.
7. No man, woman, nor child were to be seen.
8. There are plenty of molasses in the barrel.
9. He, and not I, am to blame.
10. It not only has form but life.

N. A. REVIEW.

EXERCISE XVII.

The waters slept. Night's silvery veil hung low
On Jordan's bosom, and the eddies curled
Their glossy rings beneath it, like the still,
Unbroken beating of the sleeper's pulse.
The reeds bent down the stem; the willow leaves,
With a soft cheek upon the lulling tide,
Forgot the lifting winds; and the long stems,
Whose flowers the water, like a gentle nurse,
Bears on its bosom, quietly gave way,
And leaned in graceful attitude to rest.

N. P. Willis.

Analysis.

1. How many *sentences* in the above?
2. Classify the *first* sentence.
3. Classify the *second* sentence.
4. Classify the *third* sentence.

5-18. Write all the *simple* subjects of the Exercise and after each give its *predicate-verb* or *verbs*.

State whether the following elements are *adjective* or *adverbial* in office, and on which each depends:

19. "*Night's*"; 20. "*silvery*"; 21. "*low*"; 22. "*on Jordan's bosom*"; 23. "*their*"; 24. "*beneath it*"; 25. "*down*"; 26. "*willow*"; 27. "*soft*"; 28. "*whose*"; 29. "*quietly*"; 30. "*to rest.*"

31. Of what is "*beating*" the *object*? 32. Classify "*like*."
33. Select a *participial* (or verbal) noun.
34. Select a *participial* (or verbal) adjective.
35. Is "*bent*" *transitive*? 36. Give the antecedent of "*whose.*"

EXERCISES.

37. Classify "*way.*" 38. Give its *syntax.*
39. What line is *wholly* composed of a phrase?
40. What does this phrase modify?
41. Name the verb in the *present* tense.
42. In what *tense* are the other verbs?
43. What *mood* is used throughout?
44. What *three* nouns are in the *possessive* case?
45. What pronouns are in the *possessive* case?
46. Expand "*sleeper's pulse*," using a *prepositional* phrase in place of the *possessive.*
47. Give the principal parts of "*bears.*"
48. Define an "*article.*" 49. Define a *common* noun.
50. Define a *proper* noun.

Synthesis.

1. Write a simple sentence having a noun-infinitive as the object of a verb.
2. Write a sentence composed of trisyllables.
3. Compose a complex sentence of monosyllables.
4. Form a sentence using a phrase denoting place.
5. One with a phrase denoting time.
6. Write a sentence containing a conjunctive adverb.
7. Write a complex sentence whose dependent clause expresses a condition.
8. Write a simple sentence containing two personal pronouns, one of the first, and the other of the second person.

Write separate sentences containing pronouns, as follows:
9. First, singular, common gender, possessive.
10. Second,   "   "   "   "
11. Third,   "   masculine   "   "
12. Third,   "   neuter   "   "
13. Second,   "   feminine   "   objective.
14. Third,   "   masculine   "   "
15. First, plural,   common   "   possessive.

False Syntax.

1. The boy who came last and that is now here may recite.
2. Do this for conscience's sake.
3. He will be here on to-morrow.
4. They imagined it to be she.
5. The jury is individually responsible.
6. Neither moon nor star appear in the heaven.
7. Was your scissors broken this morning.
8. It is I who is in fault.
9. The teacher tried to learn me the lesson.
10. There appears to be many more included.   BLAIR.

EXERCISE XVIII.

1. The dew was falling fast, the stars began to blink,
2. I heard a voice; it said, Drink, pretty creature, drink;
3. And looking o'er the hedge, before me I espied
4. A snow-white mountain lamb with a maiden by its side.
Wordsworth.

Analysis.

1. How many *propositions* in the above stanza?
2–3. Give the *simple subject* and *predicate* of the first one.
4–5. Give the *same* of the *second*, and
6–7. Of the *third*.
8. Which of the three verbs given are *transitive*?
9. What is the *syntactical* office of "*fast*"?   10. Of "*to blink*?"
11–12. Give the *simple subject* and *predicate* of the fourth proposition.
13. What is the object of "*said*"?
14. What is the subject of "*drink*"?

15. Of what *person* is this subject? 16. What *number?*
17. What does this subject *stand for*, or *represent?*
18. Give the *entire subject* of the last proposition.
19. Give the *entire predicate.* 20. Give the *predicate-verb.*
21. Give the *subject-nominative.*
22. What is the *object* of this verb?
23. What does "*snow-white*" modify?
24. Classify "*mountain*" as here used.
25. Of what *gender* is "*lamb*"?
26. What is the *syntactical* office of "*with a maiden by its side*"?
27. Is "*by its side*" *adjective*, or *adverbial* in office?
28. Give the corresponding opposite gender of "*maiden.*"
29. Classify "*looking.*" 30. Give its *syntactical* office.
31. What does "*and*" connect?
32. What kind of conjunction is "*and*"? 33. Compare "*fast.*"
34–38. Change the first proposition to the *other* tense forms of the *same* mood.
39. Give the principal parts of "*began.*"
40. What *independent* word occurs in the stanza?
41. Of what *person* is this word?
42. Of what *gender?* 43. In what *case?*
44. Give the principal parts of "*drink.*"
45. In what mood is "*drink*"?
46. Select an *adjective* phrase.
47. Give the rule for beginning "*Drink*" with a capital.
48. Define the *singular* number. 49. The *plural* number.
50. Define the *nominative* case.

Synthesis.

1. Write a simple sentence containing a transitive infinitive verb.
2. Write a simple sentence containing an appositive noun modified by a phrase.
3. Write a complex sentence whose subordinate clause is quoted.
4. Write a compound sentence having two dependent clauses.
5. Write a transitive imperative sentence.

Write separate sentences having the following described pronouns:

6. Third, plural, common, possessive.

7. Third, plural, common, objective.
8. Write a sentence containing a reciprocal pronoun.
9. A compound personal pronoun.
10. A compound relative pronoun.
11. A responsive (relative indefinite, indirect interrogative) pronoun.
12. *The double* relative pronoun (the one that may supply two cases).
13. Construct a sentence with *who* as a relative.
14. One with *that* as a relative.
15. One with *which* as a relative.

False Syntax.

1. He and they we know, but who art thou?
2. He spoke of Peter's the Hermit's eloquence.
3. Solomon was wiser than all men.
4. I doubted its being him.
5. The peasantry goes barefoot in some climates.
6. Thinks I to myself, I'll surprise him.
7. The young girl was very poetically.
8. Will you go, sure?
9. From the bridge quite a number of people were able to see the regatta.
10. Please step in my carriage.

EXERCISE XIX.

The Assyrian came down like the wolf on the fold,
And his cohorts were gleaming in purple and gold;
And the sheen of their spears was like stars on the sea,
When the blue wave rolls nightly on dark Galilee.
Byron.

  Lives of great men all remind us
   We can make our lives sublime,
  And departing, leave behind us
   Footprints on the sands of time.
Longfellow.

Analysis.

1. How many *sentences* in the two stanzas?
2. Classify the *first* sentence.
3. Of how many *clauses* is it composed?
4. Which clause is *dependent?*
5-12. Give the *subject-nominative* and *predicate-verb* of each clause in the first stanza.
13. What is the *syntactical* office of "*like*"?
14. What does "*on the fold*" modify?
15. What *part of speech* is "*purple*"?
16. By what is the *first* clause and the *second* connected?
17. Select an *adjective* phrase.
18. What does it modify?
19. Select an *adverbial* phrase.
20. What does it *modify?*
21. What is the syntactical office of "*on dark Galilee*"?
22. Select from the first stanza an *adverb of place.*
23. An *adverb of time.* 24. A *conjunctive* adverb.
25. Select a verb, *progressive* form.
26. Of what *gender* is "*their*"?
27. Is "*Assyrian*" a *proper* noun?
28. Is it a *collective* noun?
29. Is "*Assyrian*" singular, or *plural*, as here used?
30. Classify the *second* sentence.
31. How many *clauses* has it?
32. What is the *syntactical* office of the *second* clause?
33. Give the *entire subject* of the *first* clause.
34. Give its *entire predicate.* 35. Give its *subject-nominative.*
36. Give its *predicate-verb.*
37. What *part of speech* is "*all*"?
38. Give the *rule* for its construction.
39. Write the *possessive singular* of "*lives.*"
40. Classify "*sublime.*" 41. Classify "*departing.*"
42. To what does it relate? 43. What does "*and*" connect?
44. In what *mood* is "*leave*"? 45. In what *tense*"?
46. Give the syntax of "*on the sands of time.*"

EXERCISES. 73

47. Why does "*Footprints*" begin with a capital letter?
48. Define the *neuter* gender.   49. Define the *feminine* gender.
50. Define the *masculine* gender.

Synthesis.

1. Write a simple sentence containing a compound personal pronoun, masculine, objective.
2. A compound personal pronoun, feminine, objective.
3. Construct a sentence having the neuter compound personal pronoun in apposition with the subject.
4. A compound personal pronoun, first person, objective plural.
5. A compound personal pronoun, third person, objective plural.
6. Construct a sentence using *as* as a relative.
7. Using *what* as an interrogative pronoun.
8. Using *what* as a relative pronoun.
9. Using *what* as an adjective.
10. Using *what* as an adverb.
11. Using *what* as a noun.
12. Using *what* as an interjection.
13. Using *what* as a responsive pronoun.
14. Write a sentence with a relative pronoun referring to a joint antecedent connected by *and*.
15. Write a sentence in which the relative is *understood*.

False Syntax.

1. Five and one is six.
2. Twelve months' interest were due.
3. The wind blows very coldly to-day.
4. He experienced great trouble of writing.
5. There was none on whom I could confide.
6. The boy will fail, but he don't seem to care much.
7. John is equally wise as James.
8. Do like I do if you wish to succeed.
9. The children are into mischief.
10. O! fairest flower, no sooner blown but blasted.   MILTON.

EXERCISE XX.

1. Then came an immensely big grasshopper. However,
2. he seated himself on another rose, and rubbed his shin-
3. bone, which, strange to say, is a token of love amongst
4. grasshoppers. The rose on which he was seated did not
5. understand it, but that with the green, crippled leaf did;
6. for upon her the big grasshopper looked with eyes that
7. plainly said, I could eat thee from mere love.

Hans Christain Andersen.

Analysis.

1. How many *sentences* in the above selection?
2. How many *propositions*?
3. Which proposition is a *simple* sentence?
4. Which proposition is used *substantively* (like a noun)?
5. Select a proposition used *adjectively* (like an adjective).
6. Give the *subject-nominative* of the first sentence.
7. Give the *predicate-verb*.
8. By what is "*grasshopper*" modified?
9. What modifier has "*big*"?
10. Classify the *second* sentence.
11. Give its *principal* clause.
12. Name the clause in which "*which*" is the nominative.
13. Is this clause *adjective* or *adverbial* in office?
14. Give the antecedent of "*which*," third line.
15. What does "*amongst grasshoppers*" modify?
16. What part of speech is "*However*"?
17. Classify "*strange.*" 18. To what does it *relate*?
19. Classify "*to say.*"
20. Give the rule for its *syntactical* relation.
21. Classify the *last* sentence.

22. Write the *co-ordinate* propositions of this sentence.
23. Select the *co-ordinate* connective.
24. State what it *connects*.
25. Parse the word "*on*," fourth line.
26. Is "*was seated*" in the passive voice (passive verb)?
27. For what does "*it*" stand?
28. What *gender* is "*grasshopper*"?
29. What is the *antecedent* of "*her*"?
30. Give the *person* and *number* of "*said*."
31. Give the verb of the first proposition following "*but*."
32. Is this verb *transitive*?
33. Give its *simple* subject.
34. Select a verb having the *emphatic* form.
35. In what *tense* is this verb?
36. Select from the sixth line an *adjective* and *compare* it.
37. Select from the extract a verb in the *potential mood*.
38–40. Give its *other tense forms* in the same mood.
41. Change the last proposition to its *equivalent interrogative* form.
42. Change the same to its *equivalent passive* form.
43. What does "*from mere love*" modify?
44. What kind of conjunction is "*for*"?
45. Select an *auxiliary* verb.
46. What *property* (or *modification*) of the verb does it determine?
47. What does "*upon her*" modify?
48. Define the *first person*. 49. Define the *second* person.
50. Define the *third* person.

Synthesis.

1. Write a sentence illustrating the use of *that* as a relative pronoun.
2. *That* as an adjective pronoun.
3. *That* as a conjunction.
4. *That* as an adjective.
5. Write a sentence having a personal pronoun referring to antecedents of different persons.

Re-write the following sentences, and supply the proper relative pronouns in the blank spaces:

6. A faint tick was now heard from the pendulum —— thus spoke.
7. He spoke to the crowds —— saluted him from below.
8. The rose ———— all are praising is not the rose for me.
9. He referred to the ship and passengers —— were lost.
10. This is the sweetest flower —— blooms.
11. Pitt was the pillar —— upheld the state.
12. Are those the same stars —— came out last night?
13. Write a sentence containing a possessive relative pronoun.
14. Write a complex sentence containing a relative pronoun as the object of a preposition.
15. Write a compound sentence having a noun-clause in the objective case.

False Syntax.

1. The ship with all her crew were lost.
2. The opera was real grand.
3. They will never be no wiser.
4. The children, I fear, are lost between the crowd.
5. And so they all perished with hunger.
6. Neither the army or navy was represented.
7. You look as though you were cold.
8. The beaux of the day used the art of painting their faces, as well as the women.
9. What money he had, that was lost.
10. Hill and dale doth boast thy blessing.

EXERCISE XXI.

1. The boy stood on the burning deck,
2. Whence all but him had fled;
3. The flame that lit the battle's wreck,
4. Shone round him o'er the dead.

5. Yet beautiful and bright he stood,
6. As born to rule the storm;
7. A creature of heroic blood,
8. A proud though childlike form.
Mrs. Hemans.

Analysis.

1. How many *sentences* are comprised in the two stanzas?
2. Classify the *first* sentence.
3. Name its *leading*, or *principal*, propositions.
4–5. Name the *subordinate* propositions.
6–7. What does each subordinate *proposition* modify?
8. What *part of speech* is the first connective?
9. The *second* one?
10–13. Give the *syntactical* office of all the *prepositional* phrases in the first stanza.
14. Parse "*but.*" 15. Classify "*dead.*"
16. Give its *gender*. 17. Give its *number*.
18. Select a *participial* adjective.
19. Can this adjective be compared?
20. Give the *principal* parts of "*fled.*"
21. Of "*shone.*" 22. Of "*stood.*" 23. Of "*lit.*"
24. Classify the last stanza (as a sentence).
Give the *part of speech* and the *syntactical* office of the following elements:
25. "*Yet*"; 26. "*beautiful*"; 27. "*and*"; 28. "*bright*";
29. "*stood*"; 30. "*as*"; 31. "*born*"; 32. "*to rule*";
33. "*creature*"; 34. "*heroic*"; 35. "*proud*"; 36. "*though*";
37. "*childlike*".
38. In what mood is "*had fled*"? 39. In what *tense?*
40. Is "*beautiful*" a *predicate* adjective?
41. What word is the object of an *infinitive* verb?
42. Is "*though*" a *co-ordinate*, or a *subordinate* element?
43. Give the gender of "*creature.*"
44. Select a *simple* word.
45. Select a *derivative* word.

78 EXERCISES.

46. Select a word containing a *proper* diphthong.
47. By what is "*wreck*" modified?
48. Define a *participial* adjective.
49. Define a *numeral* adjective.
50. Define a *pronominal* adjective.

Synthesis.

1. Write a sentence containing an interrogative pronoun in the possessive case.
2. Construct a sentence containing a relative pronoun having two singular antecedents connected by *or* or *nor*.
3. Write a sentence containing a participle used as a noun.
4. A participle used as an adjective.
5. A participle used as a preposition.
6. A participle used as a conjunction.
7. A participle used as an adverb.
8. A participle used as attribute, after an intransitive verb.
9. A participle having an object, and at the same time, modified by a possessive noun or pronoun.
10. A participle modified by a possessive noun and an adverb.
11. A participle relating to a noun in the nominative absolute.
12. A participle relating to a pronoun in the nominative absolute.
13. A participle used *abstractly* after an infinitive.
14. A simple participle used as the object of a preposition.
15. The simple perfect participle changed into an adjective by prefixing the syllable *un*.

False Syntax.

1. It aint so.
2. I reckon it will rain to-day.
3. There was many giants in those days.
4. I think, if I'm not mistaken, that it rained a week ago to-day.
5. The rivers flow in two opposite directions.
6. Do you know if it is four o'clock?
7. I never was as thirsty in my life.
8. Out of the second term I took out the factor x.
9. There is ten cents for your trouble.
10. There are two hundred and forty-eight persons on board, fifty of whom have swam ashore.   N. Y. HERALD

EXERCISE XXII.

On Linden when the sun was low,
All bloodless lay the untrodden snow,
And dark as winter was the flow
 Of Iser rolling rapidly.

But Linden saw another sight,
When the drums beat at dead of night,
Commanding fires of death to light
 The darkness of her scenery.
Thomas Campbell.

Analysis.

1. How many *sentences* in the above stanzas?
2. How many *clauses*?
3. Classify the *first* sentence.
4. Classify the *second* sentence.
5. How many *principal* clauses in the Exercise?
6. How many *subordinate* (or *auxiliary*) clauses?

7-11. Write all the *prepositional* phrases and tell what each modifies.

12. Select a *participial* phrase from the first stanza.
13. What does this phrase modify?
14. What part of speech is "*all*"? 15. Give its *syntax*.
16. Select from the Exercise an *infinitive* phrase.
17. To what does it belong?
18. Give all the modifiers of "*lay*."
19. What is the simple subject of "*was*," third line?
20. Give the part of speech of "*low*."
21. What does it modify?
22. To what does "*bloodless*" belong?
23. Give the *simple* subject of "*lay*."

24. Give the principal parts of "*lay*."
25. Classify "*dark*." 26. Give its full *syntax*.
27. Parse "*as*," giving the rule.
28. Of what verb is "*winter*" the *subject?*
29. Select an *adverb of manner* and *compare* it.
30. Select an *adjective* and *compare* it.
31. Select an *abstract* noun.
32. What kind of conjunction is "*but*"?
33. Of what gender is "*Linden*" (first line)?
34. Give the gender of "*Linden*" (fifth line).

Give the *part of speech* and the *full syntactical office* of each of the following words:

35. "*Linden*," line 5; 36. "*another*"; 37. "*night*";
38. "*commanding*"; 39. "*fires*"; 40. "*to light*";
41. "*darkness*"; 42. "*scenery*."

43. Give the principal parts of "*beat*."
44. In what *mood* are all the verbs of the Exercise?
45. In what *tense?*
46. Give the *compound perfect passive* participle of "*commanding*."
47. Change the fifth line to its *corresponding passive* form.
48. Define the *comparative* degree.
49. Define the *superlative* degree.
50. Define a *verb*.

Synthesis.

1. Write a simple sentence having a transitive participial phrase as the subject of the verb.
2. A sentence using the same participle *adjectively*.
3. A sentence containing an active transitive participle, the whole phrase being used as the object of a preposition.
4. A compound perfect participle as the object of a preposition.
5. A sentence with the simple present participle used in a passive sense.
6. A compound participle as the object of a verb.
7. Write a sentence containing an *infinitive* (verb in the infinitive mood), as subject-nominative.
8. As predicate-nominative.
9. As object of a verb.

10. As object of a preposition.
11. As modifier of a subject-nominative.
12. As modifier of a predicate-nominative.
13. As modifier of the object of a verb.
14. As modifier of the object of a preposition.
15. As modifier of a predicate-adjective.

False Syntax.

1. I, and not he, is promoted.
2. Homer, as well as Virgil, were once students on the banks of the Rhine.
3. Every twig, every leaf, and every blade of grass teem with life.
4. We arrived at home safely.
5. From whence come wars?
6. The situation where he was placed was very unfortunate.
7. I only bring forward some things (tho' having others).
DEAN ALFORD.
8. Then falls huge heaps of hoary-headed walls.   DYER.
9. What is twenty-two poor years to the finishing a lawsuit?
SWIFT.
10. Meteors may be looked for if pleasant.   N. Y. TIMES.

EXERCISE XXIII.

1. She was dead. No sleep so beautiful and calm, so free
2. from trace of pain, so fair to look upon. She seemed a
3. creature fresh from the hand of God, and waiting for the
4. breath of life; not one who had lived and suffered death.
5. Her couch was dressed with here and there some winter-
6. berries and green leaves, gathered in a spot she had used
7. to favor. "When I die, put me near something that has
8. loved the light, and had the sky above it always." These
9. were her words. She was dead. Dear, gentle, patient,
10. noble Nell was dead.
Dickens.

EXERCISES.

Analysis.

1. How many *sentences* expressed or implied in the selection?
2. How many *simple* sentences?
3. How many *complex* sentences?
4. Name the *compound* sentence.
5. Which sentence is composed chiefly of adjectives?
6. Which sentence has all the parts of speech except one?
7. What pronoun is *understood* in one of the sentences?
8. Select an *adjective* clause.
9. What does this clause modify?
10. Select an *adverbial* clause.
11. Select a *relative* pronoun in the *nominative* case.
12. Give its *objective* form.
13. Select a *personal* pronoun in the *nominative* case.
14. Give its *objective form*.

Give the *part of speech* and the full *syntax* of the following words:

15. "*Dead*"; 16. "*sleep*", 17. "*beautiful*"; 18. "*upon*";
19. "*seemed*"; 20. "*creature*"; 21. "*fresh*"; 22. "*waiting*";
23. "*not*"; 24. "*one*"; 25. "*who*"; 26. "*death*";
27. "*her*"; 28. "*couch*"; 29. "*here*"; 30. "*leaves*";
31. "*gathered*"; 32. "*when*"; 33. "*put*"; 34. "*near*";
35. "*that*"; 36. "*above*"; 37. "*always*"; 38. "*Nell*."

39. In what tense is "*had lived*"?
40. In what *tense* is the verb in the ninth line?
41. Select a *perfect* (past) participle.
42. Select a verb having the *passive* form.
43. Is "*to favor*" transitive?
44. Select a *predicate-nominative*.
45. What *mood* is used throughout the Exercise?
46. Why is one of the sentences enclosed with *quotation* marks?
47. How many more *propositions* than *clauses* in the Exercise?
48. Define a verb. 49. Define a *regular* verb.
50. Define an *irregular* verb.

Synthesis.

1. Write a sentence containing an infinitive (verb in the *infinitive mood*) as the object of a participle.
2. As the object of *another* infinitive.
3. A participle as the object of an *infinitive*.
4. A noun-infinitive as an appositive of the subject.
5. An infinitive depending (by ellipsis) on a conjunction.
6. An infinitive depending on an adverb.
7. An infinitive of *purpose* depending on a verb.
8. An infinitive used *independently*.
9. Two infinitives used as joint subject of a verb.
10. A perfect infinitive passive voice (infinitive mood, perfect, passive).
11. A present infinitive progressive, transitive.
12. An infinitive with *to* omitted.
13. An infinitive taking a clause as its object.
14. Write a compound imperative sentence.
15. Write a complex interrogative sentence.

False Syntax.

1. It is his virtues, and not his wealth, that gives him honor.
2. It seems very strangely.
3. The maskers were nearly dressed alike.
4. He only spoke to me, not you.
5. They studied the lesson only, but did not learn it.
6. He very seldom or ever does so.
7. The man almost lost all his money.
8. He told us how that time is money.
9. I cannot predicate what may hereafter happen.
10. A man does not lose his mother now in the papers.

DEAN ALFORD.

EXERCISE XXIV.

1. Insist on yourself; never imitate. Your own gift you
2. can present every moment with the cumulative force of
3. a whole life's cultivation; but of the adopted talent of
4. another, you have only an extemporaneous, half posses-
5. sion. That which each can do best, none but his Maker
6. can teach him. No man yet knows what it is, nor can,
7. till that person has exhibited it. Where is the master
8. who could have taught Shakespeare? Every great man
9. is a unique.
Ralph Waldo Emerson.

Analysis.

1. How many *sentences* in the above selection?
2. Classify the *first* sentence. 3. Classify the *second*.
4. Classify the *third*. 5. Classify the *fourth*.
6–31. Write each *subject-nominative* (expressed or understood) and immediately thereafter give the *predicate-verb* agreeing with it.
32. Give the *mood* of the *first* verb of the Exercise.
33. Give the *mood* and *tense* of the *third* verb.
34. Give the *tense* of the verb in the *fourth* line.
35. Give the *mood* and *tense* of the verb in the *eighth* line.
36. Express the meaning of "*that which*" by one word.
37. Compare "*best*."
38. Give the syntax of "*but*," fifth line.
39. What does "*nor*" connect?
40. Give the part of speech and syntax of "*that*," fifth line.
41. Of "*which*." 42. Of "*what*." 43. Of "*moment*."
44. For what does "*it*" stand?

45. What *clauses* are connected by "*till*"?
46. What part of speech is "*unique*"?
47. Select a verb in the *present perfect* tense?
48. Define a conjunction.   49. Define *synopsis*.
50. Define a *transitive* verb.

Synthesis.

Write in separate sentences, and *underscore* the following elements:

1. A regular verb.   2. An irregular verb.
3. A redundant verb.   4. A defective verb.
5. A transitive verb.   6. An intransitive verb.
7. An auxiliary verb expressing emphasis.
8. A principal verb and two auxiliaries.
9. A principal verb and three auxiliaries.
10. A verb in the passive voice.
11. A verb in the active form, but having a passive meaning.
12. A verb in the passive form, but not passive in meaning.
13. A verb in the indicative present.
14. A verb in the potential past.
15. A verb in the imperative mood.

False Syntax.

1. He said nothing farther about the matter.
2. The soldier almost died for thirst.
3. I cannot deny but what he is honest.
4. I always have, and always shall be an admirer of Poe.
5. It was no other but his own brother.
6. Do you hear the whistle to blow?
7. I have not resigned, nor do I intend to.
8. I intended to have done it yesterday.
9. I seen the other boy, a throwing the stone.
10. He had broke the ice in the bucket.

EXERCISE XXV.

1. Beside yon straggling fence that skirts the way
2. With blossomed furze unprofitably gay,
3. There, in his noisy mansion, skilled to rule,
4. The village master taught his little school.
5. A man severe he was and stern to view,
6. I knew him well, and every truant knew;
7. Well had the boding tremblers learned to trace
8. The day's disasters in his morning face;
9. Full well they laughed with counterfeited glee
10. At all his jokes, for many a joke had he;
11. Full well the busy whisper circling round,
12. Conveyed the dismal tidings when he frowned.

Goldsmith.

Analysis.

1. How many *sentences* in the above extract?
2. Classify the *first* one.
3. Name its principal clause.
4. Name the *entire principal subject* of this sentence.
5. Name the *entire principal predicate*.
6. Give the *subject-nominative* and the *predicate-verb* of the *principal* clause.
7. Give the *same* of the *dependent* clause.
8. Give all the modifiers of "*fence.*"
9. Classify the *last* sentence.
10. How many *co-ordinate* propositions has it?
11. Name one *not co-ordinate*.
12. How many *propositions* has this sentence?
13. How many *clauses?*

EXERCISES. 87

14. Is a clause *always* a proposition?
15. Is a proposition *always* a clause?
16. Is the clause in line 10, *co-ordinate*, or *subordinate?*
17. Select a *conjunctive adverb*, and state what it connects.
18. Give all the modifiers of "*jokes.*"
19. Give its *modifications*, or *properties.*
20. Of what *number* and *gender* is "*school*"?

Classify and give the syntactical office of the following *elements:*

21. "*Beside*"; 22. "*yon*"; 23. "*with*"; 24. "*gay*";
25. "*there*"; 26. "*in*," line 3; 27. "*skilled to rule*"; 28. "*man*";
29. "*stern*"; 30. "*to view*"; 31. "*well*," line 7; 32. "*to trace*";
33. "*full*"; 34. "*joke*"; 35. "*well*," line 11; 36. "*circling.*"

37. Designate a verb having its object *suppressed.*
38. By what *figure of speech* is this omission known?
39. Supply the omitted word.
40. What is the tense of "*had*," line 10?
41. What *mood* is used throughout the extract?
42. Name the *tenses* represented.
43. Represent the *phonetic* spelling of "*busy.*"
44. Expand "*circling round*" into a clause.
45. Change line 4 into its *corresponding* passive form.
46. Is "*many a*" a *singular* or a *plural* expression?
47. Select a word having a *prefix* and a *suffix.*
48. Select a noun having no *singular* form.
49. Define *mood.* 50. Define *voice.*

Synthesis.

Write separate sentences embracing,

1. A verb in the indicative present.
2. In the potential present.
3. In the indicative past, emphatic form.
4. In the subjunctive present.
5. In the indicative present perfect.
6. In the potential past.
7. In the indicative past perfect.
8. In the potential present perfect, passive form.
9. In the indicative future, progressive form.

10. In the subjunctive past.
11. In the potential past perfect.
12. In the indicative future perfect, ancient form.
13. Write a sentence containing the perfect infinitive.
14. One having the compound perfect passive participle of *recite*.
15. Write a sentence containing an intransitive verb made passive by combination with a preposition.

False Syntax.

1. Take such specimens as seems proper.
2. Three and three are six, and one is seven.
3. How are each of the pronouns classified?
4. Time flies, whether we take heed or no.
5. Canteens were issued to the soldiers with short necks.
6. This will be in accordance to your ideas.
7. We should be more anxious to practice charity than of boasting of it.
8. I do not doubt but he will succeed.
9. A boy with a ripe watermelon don't speculate much on the conservation of energy.   NEWSPAPER.
10. Sometimes the editors of our papers fall from ignorance into absurd mistakes.   DEAN ALFORD.

EXERCISE XXVI.

1. How beautiful this night! the balmiest sigh
2. Which vernal zephyrs breathe in evening's ear,
3. Were discord to the speaking quietude
4. That wraps this moveless scene. Heaven's ebon vault
5. Studded with stars unutterably bright
6. Through which the moon's unclouded grandeur rolls,
7. Seems like a canopy which love has spread
8. Above a sleeping world.
                                              Shelley.

Analysis.

1. How many *sentences* in the above extract?
2. Classify the *first* sentence?
3. How many propositions in the *first* sentence?
4. Give the first *proposition* of the extract.
5. Name all the modifiers of "*sigh.*"
6. Name all the modifiers of "*quietude.*"
7. What is the object of "*breathe*"?
8. Select an adjective in the *superlative* degree.
9. Give the *mood* of "*were.*" 10. Give its *tense.*
11. Classify "*discord.*" 12. Give its *syntax.*
13. Give its *person* and *number.*
14. Can "*moveless*" be compared?
15. Classify the last sentence.
16. Give the subject-nominative and the *predicate-verb* of its *principal* proposition.
17-18. What does each *subordinate* clause modify?
19. Give all the modifiers of "*vault.*"
20. Give the entire predicate of the *principal* proposition.
21. Select an *adverbial* phrase.

Give the *part of speech* and the *syntax* of the following words:

22. "*studded*"; 23. "*with*"; 24. "*unutterably*"; 25. "*bright*"; 26. "*through*"; 27. "*moon's*"; 28. "*like*"; 29. "*above.*"

30. Give the *gender* of "*world.*"
31. Is "*world*" *singular*, or *plural*?
32. Of what *gender* is "*moon's*"?
33. Give the degree of comparison of "*bright.*"
34-38. Give the other *tense forms*, same mood, of "*has spread.*"
39. What words might take the place of "*were*"?
40. In what *mood* would the verb *then* be?
41. Give the plural possessive of "*canopy.*"
42. What kind of *adverb* is "*how*"?
43. Select an adjective *singular* number.
44. Change the last proposition to the *corresponding* passive form.
45. Select a word having a *proper* diphthong.

46. Select two words, each having *three* liquids.
47. Is "*w*" a *vowel*, or a *consonant*, in "*wraps?*
48. Define the *potential* mood. 49. Define *tense*.
50. Define a *co-ordinate* connective.

Synthesis.

1. Write a sentence in which the verb agrees with two singular subjects connected by *and*.
2. With two singular subjects connected by *or* or *nor*.
3. Write a sentence containing an *adverb of time*.
4. An adverb of *place*. 5. Of *degree*. 6. Of *manner*.
7. Of *affirmation*. 8. Of *negation*. 9. Of *doubt*.
10. Of *cause*. 11. An adverb modifying a *predicate* adjective.
12. Modifying a *passive* verb. 13. *Another* adverb.
14. Modifying a *phrase*. 15. A *proposition*.

False Syntax.

1. The girl could not spin, but desired to be taught very much.
2. I was to Boston last week.
3. Who is there in whom I can rely?
4. Rid yourself from such bad habits.
5. The tax on tea was nothing else but robbery.
6. Few cities are as grand as Paris.
7. He cannot either read nor write.
8. The oath was administered to such persons that were elected.
9. We speak that we do know.
10. A dangerous cow tossed several persons, and also plunged and tossed about the street in a formidable manner.   NEWSPAPER.

EXERCISE XXVII.

When it was winter and the snow lay all around, white and sparkling, a hare would often come jumping along and spring right over the little fir-tree. Oh! this made him so angry. But two winters went by, and when the third came, the little tree had grown so tall that the hare was obliged to run round it.

Æsop.

Analysis.

1. State the *number* of *sentences* in the Exercise.
2. Give the last word with which each proposition ends.
3. How many *propositions* in all? 4. How many *clauses*?
5. Give the *principal* proposition of the first period.
6. Give the *simple subject* of this proposition.
7. Give the *entire predicate*.
8. Name the *co-ordinate* connective in the first sentence.
9. Name the *subordinate* connective. 10. Classify the *last* sentence.
11. Give its *co-ordinate* propositions. 12. Give its *subordinate* propositions.
13. Give the *co-ordinate* connective. 14. What *propositions* does it join?
15. Give the *subordinate* connectives.
16–17. What does each *join*?
18. What is the *syntactical* office of "*but*"?
19. Select from the Exercise an *adverbial* phrase.
20. What does it modify?
21. Select a *cardinal numeral* adjective.
22. An *ordinal* numeral. 23. A *predicate-nominative*.
24. A *subject-nominative*. 25. An object of a preposition.
26. Of what *gender* is "*hare*"? 27. "*fir-tree*"?
28. What word is without *syntax*?

29. Give the four principal parts of "*lay.*"
30. Of "*come.*" 31. Of "*was.*" 32. Of "*run.*" 33. Of "*went.*"
34. What part of speech is "*all*"? 35. What does it *modify?*
36. What part of speech is "*sparkling*"?
37. What does it *modify?*
38. What part of speech is "*jumping*"?
39. Give its *full syntax* as here used.
40. What part of speech is "*right*"?
41. What does it *modify?* 42. Classify "*along.*"
43. What does it *modify?*
44. What derivative noun may be formed from "*right*"?
45. Select a verb having the *passive* form.
46. Change the last line to an *interrogative* proposition with same mood and tense.
47. Change "*But two winters went by*" to the corresponding *participial* construction.
48. Define a *conjunctive adverb.*
49. Define an *adverb of place.*
50. Define an *adverb of manner.*

Synthesis.

1. Write a sentence containing a conjunctive adverb referring to time.
2. A conjunctive adverb referring to place.
3. A conjunctive adverb referring to manner.
4. A conjunctive adverb connecting its clause to a preceding noun.
5. A conjunctive adverb connecting a noun-clause in the objective case, to the predicate of the principal proposition.
6. Compose a sentence having an interrogative adverb.
7. Having an adverb used independently.
8. Write a sentence containing a dissyllabic adverb.
9. A trisyllabic adverb. 10. A polysyllabic adverb.
11. An adverb derived from an adjective.
12. An adverb derived from a noun.
13. An adverb used in the comparative degree.
14. An adverb used in the superlative degree.
15. Write a sentence using the word "*there,*" but not as an *adverb of place.*

False Syntax.

1. Which of the two girls was the oldest?
2. It never would have availed nothing.
3. The mouth of a river is where it empties itself into some other body of water.
4. She told us they wore black ruchings a good deal now.
5. She has always been just so, ever since I knew her.
6. That wouldn't hardly do.
7. Has the last school-bell of the morning rang?
8. The two girls are of about the same age.
9. I was one day sitting on a log when I nearly fell to sleep.
10. I remember when the French band of the "Guides" were in this country reading in the *Illustrated News*.   DEAN ALFORD.

EXERCISE XXVIII.

1. On that pleasant day of the early fall,
2. When Lee marched over the mountain wall,
3. Over the mountains winding down,
4. Horse and foot into Frederick town,
5. Forty flags with their crimson bars,
6. Flapped in the morning wind; the sun
7. Of noon looked down and saw not one.

Whittier.

Analysis.

1. Classify the above sentence.
2. How many *clauses* has it?
3. Give the *predicate-verb* of the first *co-ordinate* clause.
4. Give the *simple* subject of the second *co-ordinate* clause.
5. Name the *dependent* clause.
6. Give its *connective*.   7. What does this clause modify?

8. Which lines contain no verb?
9. Which line contains a *present participle*?
10. Parse "*on*," syntactically.
11. What kind of adjective is "*that*"?
12. Give its *plural* form.
13. Compare "*pleasant*" by *prefixes*.
14. Compare "*early*" by *suffixes*.
15. What part of speech is "*when*"?
16. Give the *mood* and *tense* of "*marched*."
17. Has this verb *voice*?
18. Give your *reason* for your answer to the above.
19. Parse "*over*," third line.
20. What kind of phrase is "*winding down*" as to *form*?
21. As to its *use* or *office*?
22. What part of speech is "*down*"?
23. As what other part of speech is "*down*" frequently used?
24. Of what *gender* is "*horse*"?
25. Of what *number*? 26. In what *case*?
27. What is meant by the term "*foot*" as here used?
28. Give the plural possessive of "*foot*."
29. Parse "*into*." 30. Classify "*Frederick*."
31. What kind of adjective is "*forty*"?
32. What verb has a *compound* subject?
33. What subject has a *compound* predicate?
34. Classify "*one*." 35. Give its *syntax*.
36. What does "*not*" modify?
37. Select an *adjective* phrase.
38. Select an *adverbial* phrase.
39. Can "*crimson*" be compared?
40. In what *mood* are all the verbs?
41. In what *tense*?
42. Is "*looked*" *transitive*?
43. Change the verb in the second line to the form of the *future perfect* tense.
44. Change the last proposition to the corresponding *interrogative* form.
45. Give the rule for doubling the "*p*" in "*flapped*."
46. Select a word having three *liquids*.

47. What is the singular nominative of the pronoun "*their*," as used in the Exercise?
48. Define *mood*.   49. Define a *defective* verb.
50. Define an *auxiliary* verb.

Synthesis.

1. Write a sentence containing an *adverb* modifying a *participle*.
2. An *adverb* modifying an *infinitive*.
3. Construct a sentence containing a *preposition* having a compound object.
4. A sentence having a *complex* (or *compound*) *preposition*.
5. Write a sentence having a *preposition* following its *objective noun*.
6. Write a sentence containing a preposition whose antecedent term of relation is a *proper noun*.
7. Whose antecedent term is an *adjective*.
8. Whose antecedent term is an *adverb*.
9. Whose antecedent term is a *pronoun*.
10. Whose subsequent term (object) is an *abstract noun*.
11. Whose subsequent term is a *relative pronoun*.
12. Whose subsequent term is a *transitive infinitive*.
13. Whose subsequent term is a *participial noun*.
14. Whose subsequent term is a *clause*.
15. Write a sentence containing two *prepositions* governing the same *substantive*.

False Syntax.

1. I cannot by no means accept your kind offer.
2. They did not differ so much with each other in the beginning.
3. Every little girl of the party was dressed alike.
4. We cannot succeed without we try.
5. When will you get done with it?
6. It was done in a quiet sort of a way.
7. What have you got here?
8. Proportion is *simple* and *compound*.
9. Forbid the children enter the room.
10. The Greeks fearing to be surrounded on all sides, wheeled about and halted, with the river on their backs.   GOLDSMITH.

EXERCISE XXIX.

1. Scaling yonder peak
2. I saw an eagle wheeling near its brow;
3. O'er the abyss, his broad expanding wings
4. Lay calm and motionless upon the air,
5. As if he floated there without their aid,
6. By the sole act of his unlorded will,
7. That buoyed him proudly up. Instinctively
8. I bent my bow, yet kept he rounding still
9. His airy circle, as in the delight
10. Of measuring the ample range beneath,
11. And round about; absorbed, he heeded not
12. The death that threatened him. I could not shoot.
13. 'Twas liberty. I turned my bow aside,
14. And let him soar away. *Knowles.*

Analysis.

1. How many *sentences* in the extract?
2. Name the *simple* sentences.
3. What kind are those *not* simple?
4. What is the *entire subject* of the *first* proposition?
5. What is the *entire predicate*?
6. What are the first three words together called?
7. Expand them into a proposition *equivalent* in meaning.
8. What would the proposition so formed modify?
9. Expand "*wheeling near its brow*" into an *equivalent* proposition.
10. Would this proposition be *adjective* or *adverbial* in office?
11. What does "*o'er the abyss*" modify?
12. Give the syntax of "*motionless.*" 13. Of "*upon the air.*"

EXERCISES.

14. Give the connective of the *second* and *third* clauses.
15. What does the phrase in the fifth line modify?
16. What are the modifiers of "*will*"?
17. Give the antecedent of "*his.*" 18. Of "*their.*"
19. Give the syntax of "*proudly.*"
20. Give the syntax of the last clause of the *first* sentence.
21. Classify the *second* sentence.
22. Can "*motionless*" be compared with propriety?

Give the *part of speech* and the *syntax* of the following words:
23. "*Instinctively*"; 24. "*yet*"; 25. "*rounding*"; 26. "*still*";
27. "*circle*";   28. "*delight*"; 29. "*as,*" ninth line;
30. "*measuring*"; 31. "*beneath*"; 32. "*round*"; 33. "*about*";
34. "*absorbed*"; 35. "*that*"; 36. "*soar*"; 37. "*aside*";
38. In what *tense* are all the verbs?
39. Select a verb in the *potential* mood.
40–42. Give its *other* tense-forms of the same mood.
43. Give the *subject* of "*soar,*" if it has one.
44. Change "'*Twas liberty*" to the *corresponding interrogative-negative* form.
45. Classify the letters in "*away*" as *vowel,* or *consonant.*
46. What rule, remark, or note applies to "*soar*"?
47. Give the rules for the capitals of the Exercise.
48. Define the *imperative* mood.
49. Define the *present* tense.
50. Define, or tell how the *passive* form of a verb is made.

Synthesis.

Write separate sentences illustrating the use of *conjunctions,* as follows:

1. A co-ordinate (copulative) conjunction.
2. A subordinate conjunction.
3. A co-ordinate conjunction joining two nouns.
4. The same joining two pronouns.
5. The same joining two adjectives.
6. The same joining two adverbs.
7. A conjunction joining two prepositional phrases.
8. A conjunction joining two participial phrases.
9. A conjunction joining two infinitive phrases.

10. A conjunction joining two complex phrases.
11. A conjunction joining two compound phrases.
12. Write a sentence containing a corresponsive conjunction.
13. Write a simple sentence containing "*both——and,*" as corresponsive conjunctions.
14. A compound sentence containing the correlatives "*not only——but also.*"
15. Write a complex sentence using the correlatives "*so——that.*"

False Syntax.

1. The difference in the two brothers was slight.
2. They were expelled the society.
3. What went you out for to see?
4. I was afraid lest he would not come.
5. This book is preferable and cheaper than the other.
6. There is no doubt but the earth is spherical.
7. The river banks are much overflown.
8. It was a jewel fair and sat in gold.
9. The traveler by this time had took his seat by the lady.
10. When I hear a person use a queer expression, or pronounce a name in reading differently from his neighbors, it always goes down, in my estimation of him with a minus sign before it.
DEAN ALFORD.

EXERCISE XXX.

1. Two boys would play at chess. As there was a knight
2. short, they put a mark upon a pawn, and so made a knight
3. of him. "Hey," exclaimed the other knights, "where do
4. you come from, Mr. Clodhopper?" The boys heard the
5. scoff. "Hold your tongues," said they, "does he not per-
6. form for us just the same service as you do?"
From the German.

EXERCISES. 99

Analysis.

1. How many *sentences* in the above selection?
2. How many *propositions*?
3. Classify the *first* sentence.
4. Classify the *second* sentence.
5. Select a *declarative* proposition.
6. An *imperative* proposition.
7. An *interrogative* proposition.
8. Give the *entire* or *logical* predicate of the second sentence.
9. Give the *entire* or *logical* subject of the third sentence.
10. Select a *clause* used as a *noun*.
11. Give the *case* of this clause.
12. Select an *adjective* clause, if there is one.
13. What part of speech is "*hey*"?
14. Abridge "*As there was a knight short*" into its equivalent *participial* construction.
15. Change "*The boys heard the scoff*" to its equivalent *passive* form.
16. Give the *principal* proposition of the last sentence.
17. What is the syntactical office of "*same*"?

State whether the following phrases are *adjective* or *adverbial* in office, and on what each depends:

18. "*at chess*"; 19. "*upon a pawn*"; 20. "*of him*"; 21. "*for us.*"

Mention the *part of speech* and give the *syntactical office* of each of the following words:

22. "*As*," first line; 23. "*there*"; 24. "*short*"; 25. "*so*";
26. "*where*"; 27. "*from*"; 28. "*as*," sixth line;
29. "*knight*," first line; 30. "*hold*"; 31. "*just.*"
32. Of what *person* and *number* is "*hold*"?
33. In what *mood* is "*would play*"?
34. In what *tense*?
35. What feminine terms correspond to "*Mr.*"?
36. In what case is "*Mr. Clodhopper*"?
37. What gender is "*knight*"?
38. What gender is "*you*," last line?
39. Give the gender of "*pawn.*"

EXERCISES.

40. Give the number of "*you*," third line.
41. Represent the spelling of "*tongues*" by its elementary sounds.
42. Select a word from the first line containing a *proper* diphthong.
43. Is "*y*" a vowel, or a consonant in "*boys*"?
44. Is "*w*" a vowel, or a consonant in "*where*"?
45. What letters represent the sound of "*x*" in "*exclaimed*"?
46. Form a derivative word from "*scoff*."
47. Form an abstract noun from "*just*."
48. Define the *nominative* case.
49. Define the *possessive* case.
50. Define the *objective* case.

Synthesis.

1. Write a sentence having *as* connecting words in apposition.
2. Write a simple sentence with "*neither——nor*" as correlatives.
3. Write a sentence containing a conditional clause.
4. One containing a *causal* proposition.
5. One containing a concessive proposition.
6. Write a sentence of two clauses connected by *whether*.
7. Combine into a sentence two clauses connected by *seeing*.
8. Two clauses connected by *notwithstanding*.
9. Give an example of a sentence having two clauses subordinately connected.
10. Give one whose members are co-ordinately connected.
11. Connect two members of a compound sentence by an adversative (disjunctive) conjunction.
12. Combine in a sentence "*if——then*."
13. Construct a sentence containing a conjunction *merely introductory* in office.
14. Construct a sentence containing a comparative conjunction.
10. Write a compound sentence containing four conjunctions.

False Syntax.

1. I have had a letter wrote since yesterday.
2. Do you prefer to sing or playing?
3. I had done the problem before the teacher come in the room.
4. Try to have learned your lesson before I return.

5. The tired lambs laid down to rest.
6. The old man was setting in his easy chair.
7. Lost, a Scotch terrier, by a gentleman, with his ears cut close.
8. If I was him, I would certainly go.
9. I was just going to go.
10. The loafer seems to be created for no other purpose but to keep up the ancient order of idleness.   IRVING.

EXERCISE XXXI.

1. "Let the poison be prepared, for it is best not to linger."
2. Crito asked: "How should you like to have us bury you?"
3. Socrates replied with a smile: "Anyway you wish—if you
4. can only get hold of me. Have I not shown you, Crito,
5. that I who have been talking to you, am not the other
6. Socrates who will soon be a dead body? Do not say, then,
7. at my funeral, 'Let us bury Socrates,' for such words are
8. not only false, but they infect the soul with evil."
   Socrates.

Analysis.

1. How many *sentences* in the above extract?
2. Classify the first sentence.
3. Which is its *principal* clause?
4. Classify the *second* sentence.
5. Which clause is used *substantively?*
6. Give the *entire predicate* of the *second* sentence.
7. Classify the *third* sentence.
8. Give the *simple subject* and *predicate* of its *principal* clause.
9. Select a phrase expressing *manner.*
10. Classify the fourth *sentence.*
11. How many *clauses* has it?
12. Name its *leading* or *principal* clause.
13. Which one is *substantive* in office?

EXERCISES.

14. Name the ones that are *subordinate*.
15. State whether they are *adjective*, or *adverbial* in office.
16. What is the direct object of "*have shown*"?
17. Select a *noun* used *independently*.

Give the *part of speech* and the *syntax* of the following words:

18. "*Let*"; 19. "*be prepared*"; 20. "*for*"; 21. "*to linger*"; 22. "*how*"; 23. "*to have*"; 24. "*bury*"; 25. "*anyway*"; 26. "*if*"; 27. "*hold*"; 28. "*you*," fourth line; 29. "*that*"; 30. "*who*," fifth line; 31. "*Socrates*," sixth line; 32. "*who*," sixth line; 33. "*body*"; 34. "*then*"; 35. "*bury*," 7th line; 36. "*for*," 6th line.

37. What is the *syntax* of the clause "*you wish*"?
38. In what *mood* is the *first verb* of the Exercise?
39. Select a verb in the *potential past*.
40. Select a verb in the *present perfect* tense.
41. Select a verb *progressive* form.
42. Select a *conditional* conjunction.
43. Give the *complete* connective of the last two clauses.
44. Select a verb in the *potential present*.
45. Decline "*other*."
46. Change the last proposition so that the verb shall be in the *potential past perfect* and in the *progressive* form.
47. Select a *predicate-nominative* and decline the same.
48. Define the *passive* voice.
49. Define the *present perfect* tense.
50. Define *person* and *number* as applied to *verbs*.

Synthesis.

Write separate simple sentences giving the synopsis of the verb *teach* with *I*, through each tense of all the finite moods, using the passive-negative form, and *thou*, with the imperative.

1. Present tense,
2. Present perfect tense,
3. Past tense,
4. Past perfect tense,
5. Future tense,
6. Future perfect tense,

} Indicative mood.

7. Present tense,
8. Present perfect tense,
9. Past tense,
10. Past perfect tense,
} Potential mood.

11. Present tense,
12. Past tense,
13. Past perfect tense (if any),
} Subjunctive mood.

14. Present tense,   Imperative mood (with *thou*).

15. Write a sentence containing the negative, passive, present infinitive.

False Syntax.

1. I accuse him with dishonesty.
2. The boy looks like to his father.
3. An officer on European and Indian service are in very different situations.
4. We found the mill-stream entirely froze over and the wheel broke.
5. Our teacher said air had weight.
6. I knew him since boyhood.
7. I have been to the Exposition last year.
8. If the hat were on the hook, some one must have taken it.
9. Where did you say Pike's Peak was?
10. The lad cannot leave his father, for if he should, he would die.
BIBLE.

EXERCISE XXXII.

1. Diogenes happened to be lying in the sun; and at the
2. approach of so many people he raised himself up a little,
3. and fixed his eyes upon Alexander. The king addressed
4. him in an obliging manner, and asked him if there was
5. anything he could serve him in? "Only stand a little
6. out of my sunshine," said Diogenes. Alexander, we are
7. told, was struck with surprise at finding himself so little
8. regarded, and saw something so great in that calmness,
9. that while his courtiers were ridiculing the philosopher as
10. a monster, he said, "If I were not Alexander, I should
11. wish to be Diogenes."

Plutarch.

Analysis.

1. State the *number* of *sentences* in the extract.
2. Classify the *first* sentence.
3. Give the *entire predicate* of its *first* proposition.
4. Give the *entire predicate* of its *second* proposition.
5. Is "*happened*" transitive?   6. Compare "*many*."
7. What part of speech is "*up*"?
8. Classify the *second* sentence.
9. How many *propositions* has it?
10. Which proposition is *substantive* in office?
11. Which is *adjective* in office?
12. By what is the *adjective* clause connected to the preceding clause?
13. In what *mood* and *tense* is the verb in this clause?
14. What is the object of "*in*"?
15. What kind of conjunction is "*if*," as here used?
16. What other conjunction might be used in place of "*if*"?
17. Classify the *third* sentence.
18. Name its *principal* propositions.
19. What part of speech is "*only*"?
20. What is the nominative of "*stand*"?

EXERCISES. 105

21. Classify the *last* sentence.
22. How many *propositions* has it?

Give the *part of speech* and the *syntax* of the following elements:
23. "*to be lying*"; 24. "*at*"; 25. "*up*"; 26. "*little*," second line;
27. "*upon*"; 28. "*in*," fifth line; 29. "*little*," fifth line;
30. "*sunshine*"; 31. "*at*," seventh line; 32. "*finding*";
33. "*little*," seventh line; 34. "*regarded*"; 35. "*that*," ninth line;
36. "*monster*"; 37. "*if*"; 38. "*not*."
39. What is the object of "*said*," tenth line?
40. In what *mood* and *tense* is "*were*"?
41. Give the case of "*Alexander*."
42. Give the *mood and tense* of the verb in the last line.
43. In what case is "*Diogenes*"?
44. Is "*should wish*" *transitive*? 45. Decline "*which*."
46. Give the person and number of "*Diogenes*."
47. What is the *syntactical* use of "*as*"?
48. Define the *indicative* mood.
49. Define the *active* voice.
50. Define an *infinitive* (verb in the infinitive mood).

Synthesis.

Write separate simple sentences giving the synopsis of the verb, *sing*, with *thou*, through all the tenses of the finite moods, using the *progressive-interrogative form*.

1. Present tense,
2. Present perfect tense,
3. Past tense,
4. Past perfect tense, } Indicative mood.
5. Future tense,
6. Future perfect tense,

7. Present tense,
8. Present perfect tense,
9. Past tense, } Potential mood.
10. Past perfect tense,

11. Present tense,
12. Past tense, · } Subjunctive mood.
13. Past perfect tense (if any),

14. Present tense, Imperative mood.

False Syntax.

1. All the mens' and the boy's names were taken.
2. The bad boy hadn't ought to do it.
3. We set with our friends at the table for over an hour.
4. Had you not better lay down a while?
5. Heft it and tell me what it weighs.
6. I calculate it will rain soon.
7. That will illy accord with my notions.
8. He has fetched up agin a snag.
9. Mr. John Smith, Esq., was here this morning.
10. The Professor soon saw that the intellectual qualities of the youth were superior to those of his raiment.

MEMOIR OF JOHN LEYDEN.

EXERCISE XXXIII.

1. The skirts of the wood seemed lined with archers,
2. although a few are advanced from its dark shadow.
3. "Under what banner?" asked Ivanhoe. "Under no
4. ensign of war which I can observe," answered Rebecca.
5. "A singular novelty," muttered the knight, "to advance
6. to storm such a castle without pennon or banner dis-
7. played! Seest thou who they be that act as leaders?"
8. "A knight clad in sable armor, is the most conspicuous,"
9. said the Jewess; "he alone is armed from head to heel
10. and seems to assume the direction of all around him."
11. "What device does he bear on his shield?" replied
12. Ivanhoe. "Something resembling a bar of iron, and a
13. padlock painted blue on the black shield."

Scott, Ivanhoe.

Analysis.

1. How many *sentences*? 2. Classify the *first*.
3. What is the syntax of "*under what banner*"?
4. Of "*under no ensign*"?
5. Give the full syntax of "*which.*"
6. Decline "*which,*" and give its *case*.
7. What is the *object* of "*answered*"?
8. Give the *part of speech* and the *syntax* of "*novelty.*"
9. Give the modifiers of "*novelty.*"
10. Has "*to advance,*" case, and if so, in what case is it?
11. What *interrogative* word in line *three*?

Give the *part of speech*, the *grammatical* properties (modifications or accidents), and the *syntax* of the following words:

12-14. "*Knight*";   15-17. "*castle*";   18-20. "*seest*";
21-23. "*who*";   24-26. "*act*";   27-29. "*leaders*";
30-32. "*is armed*";   33-35. "*does bear*";   36-38. "*something.*"

39. Name all the *present* participles in the Exercise.
40. Name the *perfect* (past) participles.
41. What is the object of "*seest*"?
42. Expand "*clad in armor*" into an *equivalent* clause.
43. To what does "*around him*" belong?
44. Is "*he alone is armed*" *adjective,* or *adverbial* in office?
45. Give the *part of speech* and the *syntax* of "*blue.*"
46. Of "*what,*" eleventh line.
47. State when a collective noun takes a *singular,* and when a *plural* verb.
48. Define the *past* tense.
49. Define the *future* tense.
50. Define a *preposition.*

Synthesis.

Represent the *passive-negative* form of the sentence, "*They invite the children,*" in all the tenses of the finite moods, using the appropriate subject for the imperative.

EXERCISES.

1. Present tense,
2. Present perfect tense,
3. Past tense,
4. Past perfect tense,
5. Future tense,
6. Future perfect tense,
} Indicative mood.

7. Present tense,
8. Present perfect tense,
9. Past tense,
10. Past perfect tense,
} Potential mood.

11. Present tense,
12. Past tense,
13. Past perfect tense (if any),
} Subjunctive mood.

14. Present tense,   Imperative mood.

15. Write a sentence containing a *compound perfect passive participle*.

False Syntax.

1. Pity the poor widow woman.
2. The three friends were all of them much attached to each other.
3. Oil and water will not unite together.
4. This book is equally as interesting as the other.
5. Who first discovered the law of gravitation?
6. Please add "*tion*" to the end of the word.
7. He was completely covered over with snow.
8. My uncle presented me with a pony phaeton.
9. We saw the little flowing rivulet flowing in and out among the knolls.
10. Among all the animals upon which nature has impressed deformity and honor, there is none whom he durst not encounter.

JOHNSON.

EXERCISE XXXIV.

1. "Will you give my kite a lift?" said my little nephew
2. to his sister, after trying in vain to make it fly by drag-
3. ging it along the ground. Lucy very kindly took it up
4. and threw it into the air; but her brother neglecting to
5. run off at the same moment, the kite fell down again.
6. "Ah, now, how awkward you are!" said the little fellow.
7. "It was your fault entirely," answered his sister. "Try
8. again, children," said I. "There is an old proverb which
9. says, 'Perseverance conquers all things.'"

Charlotte Elizabeth.

Analysis.

1. How many *sentences* in the above extract?
2. Classify the *first* sentence.
3. Give the *simple* subject of its *principal* clause.
4. Give the *entire predicate* of the first sentence.
5. What is the object of "*said*"?
6. Classify the *second* sentence.
7. What word connects the clauses of this sentence?
8. In what case is "*brother*"? 9. Give its *modifiers*.
10. Classify the *third* sentence.
11. What part of speech is "*now*"?
12. Give the rule of syntax applying to "*now*."
13. Classify the *fourth* sentence.
14. Which is the *principal* proposition of this sentence?
15. Classify the *last* sentence.
16. How many *propositions* in this sentence?

EXERCISES.

Give the *part of speech* and the *syntactical office* of the following words:

17. "*Kite*"; 18. "*lift*"; 19. "*said,*" line 1; 20. "*after*";
21. "*trying*"; 22. "*to make*"; 23. "*fly*"; 24. "*dragging*";
25. "*very*"; 26. "*up*"; 27. "*to run*"; 28. "*off*";
29. "*down*"; 30. "*again*"; 31. "*said,*" 6th line; 32. "*entirely*";
33. "*try*"; 34. "*is*"; 35. "*which;* 36. "*conquers.*"

37. What noun in the Exercise is *independent* in syntax?
38. What other word has *no syntax*?
39. What adverb might be substituted for "*in vain*"?
40. What *noun* does the first "*my*" in the first line represent?
41. Answer the same question with reference to the second "*my.*"
42. Is the noun which this pronoun represents, its *antecedent*?
43. Give the mood and number of "*try.*"
44. Why is not the second word in the last line spelled "*Persevereance*"?
45. Change this line to its equivalent having the verb in the passive voice.
46. Why does "*Perseverance*" begin with a capital?
47. Give the special rule, note, or remark for the omission of "*to*" before "*fly.*"
48. Define a *compound* adjective.
49. Define *comparison.*
50. Define the *positive* degree.

Synthesis.

Write in separate sentences the six participles from the verb *recite*, designating the special name of each according to the grammar used.

1. Simple ———.
2. Simple ———.
3. Compound ——— ———.
4. Compound ——— ———.
5. Compound ——— ——— ———.
6. Compound ——— ——— ———.

EXERCISES. 111

Write in separate sentences the several infinitives (verbs in the infinitive mood) as indicated below, using the verb *recite*.
7. Present active.
8. Present passive.
9. Perfect active.
10. Perfect passive.
11. Present progressive.
12. Perfect progressive.
13. Write a sentence containing a simple participle and a perfect infinitive.
14. A compound participle and a present progressive infinitive.
15. A compound passive participle and a perfect passive infinitive.

False Syntax.

1. The boys they all went into the house.
2. We saw the new moon about the latter end of the week.
3. A squirrel can climb a tree quicker than a boy.
4. I enjoy rowing a boat about as well as anything.
5. Corporeal punishment was forbidden.
6. James was there among the rest.
7. The two first days of the week are gone.
8. I counted over five hundred ducks on the river.
9. May I get some water? I am very dry.
10. I defy any candid and clear thinker to deny in the name of inductive science either of these six propositions.

REV. JOSEPH COOK.

EXERCISE XXXV.

1. That day I oft remember, when from sleep
2. I first awaked, and found myself reposed,
3. Under a shade, on flowers, much wondering where
4. And what I was, whence thither brought, and how.
5. Not distant far from thence a murmuring sound
6. . Of waters issued from a cave, and spread
7. Into a liquid plain, then stood unmoved,
8. Pure as the expanse of heaven; I thither went
9. With unexperienced thought, and laid me down
10. On the green bank, to look into the clear
11. Smooth lake, that to me seemed another sky.
12. As I bent down to look, just opposite
13. A shape within the watery gleam appeared,
14. Bending to look on me; I started back,
15. It started back; but pleased I soon returned,
16. Pleased it returned as soon, with answering looks
17. Of sympathy and love.

Milton's Paradise Lost.

Analysis.

1. How many *sentences?* 2. Classify the *first* one.
3. Give its *entire* subject. 4. Give its *entire* predicate.
5. Name all its *subject-nominatives.*
6. Name all its *predicate-verbs.* 7. All its *objects.*
8. Name all its connectives. 9. Its *adjective* modifiers.
10. Name its *adverbial* modifiers.
11-13. What does each of its *prepositional phrases* modify?
14. What word in this sentence would not be in good taste to use in writing prose?

EXERCISES. 113

Give the *part of speech* and the *syntax* of the following words:
15. "*What*"; 16. "*wondering*"; 17. "*where*"; 18. "*thither*," line 4.
19. Classify the *second* sentence.
20. Mention its *adjective* clause.
21. Has it an *adverbial* clause? If so, name it.
22. Give the principal parts of the verb in the *ninth* line.
23. Give the *syntax* of "*distant.*"
24. What word is modified by "*far*"?
25. Compare "*far.*" 26. Give part of speech of "*thence.*"
27. *Classify* and give the *syntax* of "*unmoved.*"
28. What does "*to look*" modify?

Classify, give the *grammatical properties*, and *syntax* of the following words:
29-31. "*Sound*"; 32-34. "*stood*"; 35-37. "*expanse*", 38-40. "*me*," line 9.
41. How many *prepositions* in the last sentence?
42. Give *all* the modifiers of "*appeared.*"
43. Give all the modifiers of "*shape.*"
44. Give the *part of speech* and the *syntax* of "*opposite.*"
45 What does "*within the watery gleam*" modify?
46. Parse "*but,*" *syntactically.*
47. Give the *part of speech* and the *syntax* of "*as,*" twelfth line.
48. Define the *progressive form* and state how it is made.
49. Define an *adverb of time.*
50. Define a *conjunctive adverb.*

Synthesis.

1. Write a simple sentence containing only principal elements.
2. Add to each of these principal elements a *word* modifier.
3. To the sentence thus formed add two phrase modifiers.
4. To the sentence last formed add a clause modifier.
5. Write a transitive infinitive phrase.
6. Construct a sentence using this phrase *adjectively.*
7. A sentence using it *adverbially.*
8. A sentence using it *substantively.*

9. Write a sentence containing *post-master-general* in the possessive plural.

10. Write a simple sentence containing a derivative and a primitive dissyllable.

11. Write a sentence containing a compound noun, a compound adjective, and a compound preposition.

12. Write a sentence illustrating the use of the hyphen and the apostrophe.

13. Write a correct elliptical sentence.

14. Write a sentence accompanied by an interjection of sorrow.

15. Write a sentence containing an adjective of irregular comparison, in the superlative degree.

False Syntax.

1. Try to set up or I'll sit you up.
2. I guess this ere will half to do.
3. Had I've been there, all would have been well.
4. The dying and expiring soldier bid his comrades farewell.
5. He is as cross as a setting hen.
6. I love chops and tomato sauce.
7. The children were raised in a Christian home.
8. The soldiers being repulsed, flew to the rear.
9. The death of his son greatly effected him.
10. It belonged to that peculiar class of poetry which never has, and never will awaken sympathy in the universal heart.

N. A. REVIEW.

EXERCISE XXXVI.

1. The boat had touched this silver strand,
2. Just as the hunter left his stand,
3. And stood concealed amid the brake,
4. To view this lady of the lake.
5. The maiden paused as if again
6. She thought to catch the distant strain.
7. With head up-raised, and look intent,
8. And eye and ear attentive bent,
9. And locks thrown back, and lips apart,
10. Like monument of Grecian art,
11. In list'ning mood, she seemed to stand,
12. The guardian naiad of the strand.

Scott, Lady of the Lake.

Analysis.

1. Of how many *sentences* is the above extract composed?
2. Select a *simple* sentence.
3. Select a *complex* sentence.
4. How many *clauses* in the first sentence?
5. How many *propositions* ?
6. What is the *entire* or *logical subject* of the first sentence?
7. What is the *entire* or *logical predicate* ?
8. What is the *subject-nominative* ?
9. What is the *predicate-verb* ?
10. Parse the *connective* in the *fifth* line.
11. Give the *entire* or *logical predicate* of the last sentence.
12. Give its *predicate-verb*.
13. In what *case* is "*naiad*"? 14. Of what *gender* ?
15. What modifiers has "*naiad*"?

EXERCISES.

Write each of the following words, give its *classification*, and state its *full syntax* as used in the extract:

16. *"Boat";*   17. *"had touched";* 18. *"silver";*   19. *"just";*
20. *"concealed";* 21. *"to view";*   22. *"this";*   23. *"lake";*
24. *"again";*   25. *"to catch";*   26. *"strain";*   27. *"up-raised";*
28. *"look";*   29. *"intent";*   30. *"attentive";* 31. *"bent";*
32. *"apart";*   33. *"monument";* 34. *"Grecian";* 35. *"art."*

36. Between what does "*with*" show the relation?
37. What does "*in listening mood*" modify?
38. Give the *mood* of "*had touched.*" 39. Give the *tense.*
40. Change the first line to its equivalent *interrogative* form.
41. Give the corresponding opposite gender of "*hunter.*"
42. Is "*thought*" a *transitive* verb as here used?
43. What *part of speech* is not found in the extract?
44. Give the rule for the beginning of "*Grecian*" with a capital.
45. Select a *compound* word.
46. Of what noun is "*maiden*" the *feminine ?*
47. Do adjectives in English *usually follow*, or *precede*, their nouns?
48. Define an *adjective.*
49. Define a *descriptive* (or *common*) adjective.
50. Define a *definitive* (or *limiting*) adjective.

Synthesis.

Write appropriate sentences exhibiting the various pronouns and their declined forms, as indicated below:

1. In one sentence, the three cases of *I* in the singular number.
2. The three cases or forms of *thou* in the singular number.
3. The three cases of *you.*
4. The three cases of *we.*
5. The three cases of *ye.*
6. The three cases of *they.*
7. The three cases of *he.*
8. The three cases of *she.*
9. The three cases of *it.*
10. The nominative and the possessive case of *who.*

11. The possessive and the objective case of *who*.
12. The nominative and the objective case of *which*.
13. The nominative and the possessive case of *which*.
14. The nominative and the possessive case of *that*.
15. The possessive and the objective case of *that*.

False Syntax.

1. We expected that our friends would have come.
2. The old ruins which we visited appears to be a very fine building.
3. The subject of a verb ought to be in the nominative case.
4. Be that as it shall, I cannot go.
5. Who should I meet the other day but my old friend, Mr. Smith.
6. The little child was drownded.
7. Passing into the room he hanged his hat on a nail.
8. I trust I shall get the better of my illness.
9. He was that poor he could not pay his rent.
10. A vehicle would have been broken to pieces in a deep rut, or come to grief in a bottomless pit. Dean Alford.

EXERCISE XXXVII.

1. Do you hear the children weeping, O my brothers!
2. Ere the sorrow comes with years?
3. They are leaning their young heads against their mother's,
4. And that cannot stop their tears.
5. The young lambs are bleating in the meadows,
6. The young birds are chirping in the nest,
7. The young fawns are playing in the shadows,
8. The young flowers are blooming from the west;
9. But the young, young children, O my brothers!
10. They are weeping bitterly!
11. They are weeping in the playtime of the others,
12. In the country of the free.
Mrs. Browning.

Analysis.

1. How many *sentences* in the above stanza?
2. Classify the *first* sentence.
3. Give its *principal* clause.
4. Give the *entire* predicate of this sentence.
5. What word connects the clauses?
6. In what *case* is "*brothers*"?
7. Classify the *second* sentence.
8–11. Give the *grammatical subject* and *predicate* of each of its clauses.
12. What is the *syntax* of "*against their mother's*"?
13. In what *case* is *heads*"?
14. In what *mood* is the verb in the *third* line?
15. The verb in the *fourth* line?
16. What part of speech is "*that*"?
17. What does it *stand for*, or *represent*?
18. Classify the *third* sentence.
19. How many *propositions* compose this sentence?
20. Are any of them *subordinate*?
21. What line contains a *conjunction*, but no *verb*?
22. What line contains only a *phrase*?
23. What does this phrase *modify*?
24. Contract it into a *simple* phrase.
25. Abridge to a simple phrase, "*in the playtime of the others.*"
26. Select the verbs having the *progressive* form.
27. How is the *progressive form* made?
28. What verb has the *emphatic* form?
29. Does this verb express *emphasis*?
30. In what case is "*mother's*"?
31. What does it *possess*?
32. Give the gender of "*lambs.*"
33. Of "*their.*" 34. Of "*fawns.*"
35. What does "*but*" connect?
36. In what case is "*children,*" ninth line?
37. Select an *adjective* phrase.
38. What part of speech is "*weeping*"?
39. To what does it relate?

EXERCISES. 119

40. Select an interjection (exclamation).
41. An *adverb of manner*. 42. An *adverb of negation*.
43. What is the name of the participle in "*ing*"?
44. Select a word having two *improper* diphthongs.
45. Of what *person* is "*brothers*"?
46. Represent the spelling of "*of*" by its *elementary* sounds.
47. Decline "*others*" in the singular and the plural.
48. Define the *nominative* case.
49. Define the *possessive* case.
50. Define the *objective* case.

Synthesis.

1. Write in a sentence the pronoun *whoever*.
2. The pronoun *whichever*.
3. The pronoun *whatever*.
4. The pronoun *whomsoever*.
5. The pronoun *whichsoever*.
6. The pronoun *whatsoever*.
7. The pronoun *whosesover*.
8. The nominative and the possessive case of *one*, singular number.
9. The possessive and the objective case of *other*, singular number.
10. The nominative and the possessive case of *one*, plural number.
11. The pronoun, *himself*, in the nominative case.
12. The pronoun, *herself*, in the objective case.
13. The pronoun, *itself*, in the objective case.
14. The pronoun, *themselves*, in the nominative case.
15. Write a compound sentence containing two relative and three personal pronouns.

False Syntax.

1. The lady was an administrator.
2. The canary is a very fine songstress.
3. A dissyllable is where two syllables are united.
4. She is the best poet of the lady writers.
5. He was necessitated from participating.
6. Either the young man or his friends has acted with imprudence.

7. I reckon that is a right smart chance.
8. Cyrus did not wait for the Babylonians coming to attack him.
ROLLIN.
9. Adversity both taught you to think and to reason.   STEELE.
10. The greatest masters of critical learning differ among one another.
SPECTATOR.

EXERCISE XXXVIII.

1. Now there was not far from the place where they lay a
2. castle called Doubting Castle, the owner whereof was
3. Giant Despair, and it was in his grounds they now were
4. sleeping; wherefore he, getting up in the morning early,
5. and walking up and down in his fields, caught Christian
6. and Hopeful asleep in his grounds. Then with a grim
7. and surly voice, he bade them awake, and asked them
8. whence they were, and what they did in his grounds.
9. They told him they were pilgrims, and that they had lost
10. their way. Then said the Giant, "You have this night
11. trespassed on me by trampling and lying on my ground,
12. and therefore you must go along with me."
John Bunyan.

Analysis.

1. Classify the *first* sentence.
2. How many *propositions* has it?

Classify and give the *syntax* of the following elements :

3. "*Now*";   4. "*there*";   5. "*was*," line 1;   6. "*not*";   7. "*far*";
8. "*from the place*";   9. "*where*";   10. "*castle*";
11. "*called*";   12. "*Doubting Castle*";   13. "*whereof*";
14. "*Giant Despair*";   15. "*in his grounds*," line 3;   16. "*wherefore*";
17. "*getting*";   18. "*up*," fourth line;   19. "*down*";   20. "*early*";
21. "*in*," fifth line;   22. "*asleep*";   23. "*in his grounds*," sixth line.

24. Classify the *second* sentence.
25. Give the number of propositions in it.
26. Give the *simple subject* and *predicate* of the first one.
27. Classify "*awake*" and give its *syntax*.
28. Give the *direct* object of "*asked.*"
29. Give the rule for parsing "*them,*" seventh line.
30. Give the *syntax* of "*Then,*" line 6.
31. Give the principal parts of "*bade.*"
32. What is the syntactical office of "*whence they were*"?
33. What part of speech is "*what*"? 34. Give its *syntax*.
35. What does "*and*" connect, eighth line?
36. Classify the *third* sentence.
37. What is the *object* of "*told*"?
38. Classify the *last* sentence.
39. What is the *object* of "*said*"?
40. Give the syntax of "*night.*"
41. Give the syntax of "*lying.*"
42. What connects the *last* clause to the one preceding?
43. What is the syntax of "*therefore*"?
44. Why is "*You*" (tenth line) capitalized?
45. Give the *mood* and *tense* of the last verb of the Exercise.
46. Give the syntax of "*along*".
47. Select a verb in the *present perfect* tense.
48. Define an *intransitive* verb. 49. Define a *principal* verb.
50. Define an *auxiliary* verb.

Synthesis.

1. Write a simple sentence having the verb transitive.
2. Add to this sentence an adjective clause modifying the subject.
3. To the sentence last formed, add an adverbial clause.
4. Make the last sentence compound by adding one co-ordinate member.
5. Further develop the sentence by adding to the second co-ordinate member an adjective clause.
6. Write a sentence containing "*methinks.*"
7. Write a sentence in which *a* is a preposition.

8. In which *a* modifies a possessive noun.
9. In which *all* is an adverb.
10. In which *also* is an adverb.
11. In which *also* is a conjunction.
12. In which *as* is a pronoun.
13. In which *as* is a preposition.
14. In which *as* is an adverb.
15. In which *as* is a conjunction.

False Syntax.

1. Give the balance of our dinner to Tommy, our cat.
2. I carried the corn to mill in the horse and waggon.
3. He sent a good deal of fat cattle to New York.
4. The bird flew out the window.
5. Was I to inform the teacher you would be punished.
6. His future prospects are right good.
7. Tom's a brick with a gilt edge.
8. The young man's anticipations of the future were of the gloomiest character.
9. Two or more sentences united together is called a compound sentence. DAY'S GRAMMAR.
10. That fertile source of mistakes among our clergy, (is) the mispronunciation of Scripture proper names. DEAN ALFORD.

EXERCISE XXXIX.

1. Ah! who can tell how hard it is to climb
2. The steep where Fame's proud temple shines afar;
3. Ah! who can tell how many a soul sublime
4. Has felt the influence of malignant star,
5. And waged with Fortune an eternal war;
6. Check'd by the scoff of Pride, by Envy's frown,
7. And Poverty's unconquerable bar,
8. In life's low vale remote has pined alone,
9. Then dropt into the grave unpitied and unknown!

10. And yet the languor of inglorious days,
11. Yet equally oppressive is to all;
12. Him, who ne'er listened to the voice of praise,
13. The silence of neglect can ne'er appal.
14. There are, who, deaf to mad Ambition's call,
15. Would shrink to hear the obstreperous trump of Fame,
16. Supremely blest, if to their portion fall,
17. Health, competence and peace. Nor higher aim
18. Had he, whose simple tale these artless lines proclaim.

Beattie.

Analysis.

1. How many *sentences* in the above stanzas?
2. Classify the *first* one.
3. How many *clauses* does it contain?
4. *Classify* and give the *syntax* of the following words:

5. "*Who*," line 1; 6. "*hard*"; 7. "*to climb*"; 8. "*where*";
9. "*afar*"; 10. "*Checked*"; 11. "*bar*"; 12. "*remote*";
13. "*dropt*"; 14. "*unknown*"; 15. "*languor*"; 16. "*him*";
17. "*are*"; 18. "*who*," line 14; 19. "*deaf*"; 20. "*to hear*";
21. "*blest*"; 22. "*if*"; 23. "*peace*"; 24. "*aim*";
25. "*whose*"; 26. "*tale*."

27. What classes of words are compared?
28. Give an *example* of each class, and *compare* the example given.
29. Make a list of all the *proper* nouns in the exercise.
30. Why are *these* nouns *proper?*
31. Give the gender of *"Fortune."*
32. Of *"Ambition's."*
33. What *moods* are represented?
34. What *tenses?*
35. Give the antecedent of *"their,"* line 16.
36. What is the object of *"can tell,"* line 3?
37. Give the *properties* (*modifications*) of *"soul."*
38. Give all the *modifiers* (*adjuncts*) of *"soul."*
39. Give the tense of *"waged."*
40. Change the last proposition to its *equivalent passive* form.
41. Select a word having a *silent* consonant.
42. *Classify* and give the *syntax* of *"yet,"* line 10.
43. Give the *syntax* of *"yet,"* line 11.
44. Explain why the sentence beginning with *"who,"* does not end with an *interrogation* point?
45. Give all the *perfect participles* in the Exercise, used alone as *such*.
46. Select an *adjective* from which an abstract noun may be formed, and *decline* this *noun*.
47. Select a *polysyllabic* adjective, from its primitive form a *noun* and write its *possessive plural*.
48. Define an *adverb of place*.
49. Define an *adverb of manner*.
50. Define an *adverb of degree*.

Synthesis.

1. Write a sentence containing a descriptive and a definitive adjective.
2. A common, a proper, and a collective noun.
3. An adjective element, and an adverbial element.
4. A word modifier, a phrase modifier, and a clause modifier.
5. An adjective phrase, an adverbial phrase, and a substantive phrase.

6. A prepositional phrase, a participial phrase, and an infinitive phrase.

7. A simple, a complex, and a compound phrase.

8. Write a sentence accompanied by an independent phrase.

9. Write a complex sentence with the verb in the principal clause in the potential mood; the other verb, in the subjunctive.

10. Write a sentence having a noun in apposition with a proposition.

11. Write a simple sentence containing all the parts of speech.

12. Write a simple sentence containing the words *to, too,* and *two.*

13. Write a sentence containing a day of the week, a month of the year, and a season of the year, being careful to capitalize correctly.

14. Write in a sentence the words, *city, county,* and *state,* prefixing to each an appropriate proper noun—or let the name come after, being connected by the word *of.*

15. Write a simple sentence containing a *comparative* adjective, and also *but* as a preposition.

False Syntax.

1. We attackted the army, at daylight, and the charge was very effective.

2. How many spoonsful make two cupsful?

3. He is a kinder good feller after all.

4. In sunshine, storm, and in tempest, he was always the same.

5. It is a general time of plenty and crops are excellent.

6. The settler there the savage slew.

7. The opera will be here about the latter end of the week.

8.   Ere you remark another's sin,
      Bid thy conscience look within.   GAY.

9. He is wiser than me.   DEAN ALFORD.

10. If with your inferiors, speak no coarser than usual; if with your superiors, no finer.   ID.

EXERCISE XL.

1. Then the servants, at Captain John Hull's command,
2. heaped double handfuls of shillings into one side of the
3. scales, while Betsey remained in the other. Jingle, jingle,
4. went the shillings, as handful after handful was thrown
5. in, till plump and ponderous as she was, they fairly
6. weighed the young lady from the floor.
7. "There, son Samuel," said the honest mint-master,
8. resuming his seat in his Grandfather's chair, "Take these
9. shillings for my daughter's portion. Use her kindly, and
10. thank Heaven for her. It is not every wife that's worth
11. her weight in silver."

Hawthorne.

Analysis.

1. How many *sentences* in the above extract?
2. Classify the *first* one.
3. Give its *principal* clause.
4. What is the *syntactical* office of the *dependent* clause?
5. What part of speech is the *last* word of the first sentence?
6. Give the *syntax* of "*at Captain John Hull's command.*"
7. Of "*into one side of the scales.*"
8. Classify the *second* sentence.
9. How many *subordinate* clauses has it?
10. Is the *second* subordinate clause *adjective* or *adverbial* in office?
11. What does "*after handful*" modify?
12. Give the *tense* and *voice* of "*was thrown.*"
13. Is "*weighed*" *transitive?*
14. Classify the *last sentence.*
15. How many *clauses* has it?
16. What is the object of "*said*"?

EXERCISES.

17. In what *mood* and *tense* is "*use*"?
18. What is the subject of "*thank*"?
19. Give the rule for parsing "*wife.*"
20. Give the rule for parsing "*worth.*"
21. Has "*it*" an *antecedent*?

Give the *part of speech* and the *syntax* of the following words:

22. "*Then*"; 23. "*double*"; 24. "*while*"; 25. "*jingle*";
26. "*as*," fourth line; 27. "*plump*"; 28. "*as*," fifth line;
29. "*from*"; 30. "*there*"; 31. "*son*"; 32. "*Samuel*";
33. "*in*," eighth line; 34. "*for*," ninth line; 35. "*worth.*"
36. Express the *feminine plural* of "*servant.*"
37. Is the plural of "*handful*" properly formed in the Exercise?
38. Give the part of speech of "*in*," fourth line.
39. What two words in the Exercise express corresponding opposite genders?
40. Of what gender is "*Heaven*"?
41. Select a *plural* adjective.
42. When is a *collective* noun of other than the neuter gender?
43. Of what *gender* is a collective noun when it is plural in *form*?
44. Give a list of all the *proper* diphthongs in the language.
45. What *moods* are represented in the Exercise?
46. What *tenses*?
47. Give the possessive plural of "*attorney-general.*"
48. Define the *emphatic* form of a tense.
49. What are *forms of a tense*?
50. Define a *participle*.

Synthesis.

1. Write a sentence containing the comparative *than.*
2. Write a sentence containing *than* as a preposition.
3. Write a complex sentence containing two adverbial clauses of time.
4. Form an interrogative sentence with the pronoun in the objective case.
5. Form a complex sentence whose subordinate proposition shall express *cause.*

EXERCISES.

6. Form a sentence containing an indirect object.
7. Form a question-sentence, with the interrogative pronoun in the possessive case.
8. Write a sentence containing the possessive plural of *mother-in-law.*
9. Of *aid-de-camp.*   10. Of *billet-doux.*
11. Of *habeas-corpus.*   12. Of *half-penny.*
13. Of *sloop-of-war.*
14. Write a simple sentence that cannot be put into the interrogative form without changing the mood of the verb.
15. Write a sentence containing the moods that may be used in interrogative sentences.

False Syntax.

1. I do not know who you mean.
2. Hoist me down in the coal mine.
3. Whether you conform to the rule, we cannot admit you.
4. The committee's rebuke had the effect intended.
5. Of a pleasant morning we often walk out in the fields.
6. The farmer grows his own cattle and drives them to market.
7. If twenty-four cents will buy six oranges, how much will forty-eight cents buy?
8. The foreigner could neither read nor write.
9. The defects in our present system are apparent.
                                        UNIVERSITY STUDENT.
10. No monstrous height, or length, or breadth appear.   POPE.

EXERCISE XLI.

1. Heaven from all creatures hides the book of fate,
2. All but the page prescribed, their present state;
3. From brutes what men, from men what spirits know:
4. Or who could suffer being here below?
5. The lamb thy riot dooms to bleed to-day,
6. Had he thy reason would he skip and play?
7. Pleased to the last, he crops the flowery food,
8. And licks the hand just raised to shed his blood.
9. Oh, blindness to the future! kindly given,
10. That each may fill the circle marked by Heaven
11. Who sees with equal eye, as God of all,
12. A hero perish, or a sparrow fall,
13. Atoms or systems into ruin hurl'd,
14. And now a bubble burst and now a world.

Pope's Essay on Man.

Analysis.

1. Classify the *first* sentence.
2. How many *propositions* has it?
3. What word supplies the *ellipsis* in the third line?
4. What kind of pronoun is "*what*"?
5. To what is it *equivalent?*
6. What part of speech is the antecedent part of "*what*"?
7. Give the part of speech of "*all*" in the *first* and in the *second* line.
8. Give the *number* and *gender* of "*all*," second line.

Give the *part of speech* and the *syntax* of the following words:

9. "*From,*" first line; 10. "*All,*" second line; 11. "*but*";
12. "*prescribed*"; 13. "*state*"; 14. "*from,*" third line
15. first "*what*"; 16. first "*men*"; 17. "*Or,*" line 4.
18. "*being*"; 19. "*here*"; 20. "*below.*"

21. Classify the *second* sentence.
22. Give its *leading* or *principal* clause.
23. In what case is "*lamb*"?
24. What is the object of "*dooms*"?
25. In what case is "*to-day*"?
26. Is the proposition in the fifth line *adjective* or *adverbial* in office?
27. Answer the same of the *first* proposition of the sixth line.
28. Give the *mood* and *tense* of "*would skip*."
29. Give the *mood* and *tense* of "*Had*."
30. Classify the *third* sentence.
31. Give its *entire subject*. 32. Give its *entire predicate*.
33. Select from this sentence a *participle* and an *infinitive*.
34. Classify each of them.
35. Classify the *last* sentence.
36. Give its *principal* clause.
37. Give its *subordinate* clauses.
38. Are any words *understood* in this sentence?
39. Give the syntax of "*blindness*." 40. Of "*given*."
41. Classify "*Heaven*." 42. Give its *gender*.
43. Give the *part of speech* and *syntax* of "*God*."
44. Of "*sparrow*." 45. Of "*fall*."
46. Between what does "*into*" show the relation?
47. Give the *syntax* of "*burst*."
48. Define a *modifier*. 49. An adjective *modifier*.
50. Define an *adverbial* modifier.

Synthesis.

1. Write a simple sentence containing two predicate adjectives.
2. With a compound word as the object of a preposition.
3. Compose a simple sentence containing the words *I* and *O*.
4. One containing two primitive dissyllables.
5. Write a simple sentence containing a modified objective element.
6. Containing two phrase objective elements.
7. An adjective clause connected by *when*.
8. A substantive clause as the object of a participle.

9. A substantive clause as the object of an infinitive.
10. A substantive clause as the object of a preposition.
11. Write a sentence with *worth* as a noun.
12. With *worth* as an adjective.
13. With *worth* as a preposition.
14. Write a sentence, expressing a *threat* or *determination*, using *I* as subject.
15. Write a sentence containing an adjective modifying two nouns.

False Syntax.

In this and in the following exercises, one sentence of the last five is CORRECT.

1. The old warrior was bred and born in New Hampshire.
2. As far as I can see, the point is well taken.
3. No less than fifty dollars were paid for what was not worth twenty.
4. We cannot afford such another victory.
5. You may call upon me at about three o'clock in the afternoon.
6. I want to go to the concert the worst way.
7. The vessel is off Cape Ann or thereabouts.
8. Wanted to adopt two children, who will be treated as one of the family.
9. May they not perform the task equally as well?
10. Scotland and thee did each in other live. DRYDEN.

11. You had best not anger me, if you would go in peace.
12. He had traveled both in Europe, in Africa, and in America.
13. 'Twas Love's mistake who fancied what it feared.
14. The world will rest content with such poor things as you and me.
MAGAZINE.
15. "You are always coming to tea now-a-days, Robert," he said. "I should think you had drunk enough tea in China."
HENRY JAMES, JR.

EXERCISE XLII.

1. Flag of the brave! thy folds shall fly,
2. The sign of hope and triumph, high.
3. When speaks the signal trumpet-tone,
4. And the long line comes gleaming on;
5. Ere yet the life-blood, warm and wet,
6. Has dimmed the glistening bayonet,
7. Each soldier eye shall brightly turn
8. To where thy sky-born glories burn;
9. And as his springing steps advance,
10. Catch war and vengeance from the glance.
11. And when the cannon-mouthings loud
12. Heave in wild wreaths the battle-shroud,
13. And gory sabres rise and fall
14. Like shoots of flame on midnight's pall,
15. Then shall thy meteor glances glow,
16.   And cowering foes shall sink beneath
17. Each gallant arm that strikes below
18.   The lovely messenger of death.

Drake.

Analysis.

1. Classify the *first* sentence.
2. Classify the *second* sentence.
3. Classify the *third* sentence.
4. Give the *number* and *case* of "*flag.*"
5. Give the grammatical properties of "*brave.*"

6–17. Write all the *subject-nominatives* of the stanza, and immediately after each give its *predicate-verb.*

EXERCISES.

Give the *part of speech* and the *syntax* of the following words:

18. "*Sign*"; 19. "*high*"; 20. "*When*," line 3; 21. "*gleaming*";
22. "*on*," line 4; 23. "*Ere*"; 24. "*yet*"; 25. "*Each*," line 7;
26. "*To*"; 27. "*where*"; 28. "*And*," ninth line; 29. "*from*";
30. "*when*," eleventh line; 31. "*like*"; 32. "*on*," fourteenth line;
33. "*Then*"; 34. "*beneath*"; 35. "*below*"; 36. "*messenger*."
37. In what *mood* are all the verbs?
38. What *tenses* are represented?
39. What is the *syntax* of the clause in the ninth line?
40. Of what *gender* is "*line*"?
41. In what *tense* is "*catch*"?
42. What is meant by "*the lovely messenger of death*"?
43. Select an *adjective* clause.
44. Select all the *participial* adjectives of the Exercise.
45. Give the *antecedent* of "*thy*," fifteenth line.
46. What *preposition* has a *compound* object?
47. What *verb* has a *compound* object?
48. Define the *perfect* (or past) *participle*.
49. Define the *past perfect* tense.
50. Define *conjugation*.

Synthesis.

1. Write a sentence containing *what* as a double relative, in two cases—nominative and objective.
2. Write a simple sentence with *what* as a predicate-nominative, and at the same time as the object of a preposition.
3. Accompany a simple sentence with *what* as an interjection.
4. With *what* as an anverb.
5. Write a simple sentence containing the adjective *beautiful* modifying the subject.
6. Change the proposition thus formed into a complex sentence by expanding the *adjective* into an *equivalent* clause.
7. Express in a sentence the superlative degree of an adjective of irregular comparison.
8. Write in a sentence an adjective having no positive degree.
9. An adjective having no comparative.

EXERCISES.

10. An adjective having neither positive nor superlative.
11. One of the superlatives of *out*.
12. Write a sentence having a suitable infinitive following *ought* considered as a *past* tense.
13. Write a sentence in which there is an ellipsis of *which*.
14. Write a sentence in which two negatives are correctly used to express an affirmative.
15. Write a sentence in which four rules for capitals shall be illustrated.

False Syntax.

1. This will not do by any manner of means.
2. Give it to the six successful students or either of them.
3. She displayed a mighty destitution of capacity.
4. I expect he must have arrived last night.
5. When did you come in town?
6. Next week a Thursday is the Fourth of July.
7. Tell me in sadness whom is she you love?   SHAKESPEARE.
8. Whereunto the righteous fly and are safe.   BARCLAY.
9. Their intermediate forms must be looked only for in the poets.
    OSCAR SCHMIDT.
10. *Iago.* He's married.
    Cassio. To who?   SHAKESPEARE.

---

11. The prisoner was not only accused of robbery but of treason.
12. Father and I dug potatoes from early morn till eve.
13. Those persons who but speak to display their wisdom are unworthy of attention.
14. He dare not touch a hair of Catiline.
15. I am the general who command you.

EXERCISE XLIII.

1. A story, in which native humor reigns,
2. Is often useful, always entertains;
3. A graver fact, enlisted on your side,
4. May furnish illustrations well applied;
5. But sedentary weavers of long tales
6. Give me the fidgets, and my patience fails.
7. 'Tis the most asinine employ on earth,
8. To hear them tell of parentage and birth,
9. And echo conversations, dull and dry,
10. Embellished with—"He said," and "So said I."
11. At every interview their route the same,
12. The repetition makes attention lame;
13. We bustle up with unsuccessful speed,
14. And in the saddest part cry—"Droll indeed!"
15. A great retailer of this curious ware,
16. Having unloaded and made many stare,
17. "Can this be true?" an arch observer cries,
18. "Yes (rather moved), I saw it with these eyes."
19. "Sir! I believe it on that ground alone;"
20. I could not, had I seen it with my own."

Cowper.

Analysis.

1. How many *sentences* in the above Exercise?
2. Classify the *first* one.
3. Give the entire subject of the *first principal* clause.
4. Give its *entire predicate*.
5. Give the entire subject of the *second principal* clause.
6. Classify the *second* sentence.

EXERCISES.

7. Give its *entire* subject.
8. Give its *entire* predicate.

Give the *part of speech* and the *syntax* of the following words:

9. "*Employ*"; 10. "*To hear*"; 11. "*echo*"; 12. "*Embellished*";
13. "*route*"; 14. "*same*"; 15. "*lame*"; 16. "*indeed*";
17. "*made*"; 18. "*stare*"; 19. "*rather*"; 20. "*moved*";
21. "*alone*"; 22. "*own.*"

23. Name all the *substantive* clauses in the Exercise, expressed or implied.
24. Is either "*said*" *transitive?*
25. What does the *prepositional* phrase in line 11 modify?
26. What kind of adverb is "*so*"?
27. Classify the *last* sentence.
28. Select its *subordinate* proposition.
29-31. Mention each *verb* of this sentence, and give its *simple subject* and its *object*, if it has one.
32. Give the rule for parsing "*retailer.*"
33. Give its *modifications*, or *properties*.
34. Give its *modifiers*.
35. Give the *mood* and *tense* of the last verb in the last line.
36. Give the *same* of the *first* verb in the last line.
37. Give the *part of speech* and *modifications* of "*Sir.*"
38. Parse "*Yes,*" and give the rule or note.
39. Select a *compound* participle.
40. Select a *plural objective pronoun* and give its *antecedent*.
41. Give the *modifiers* of "*conversations.*"
42. Select *three adjectives* each representing a different degree of comparison.
43. Give the *synopsis* of the last *verb* of the Exercise, preserving its *mood* and using your own *name* as *subject*.
44. Select an adjective of the *superlative* degree and change it into an *adverb* of the *same* degree.
45. What ellipsis *may* be supplied in the sixth line?
46. Form a *compound perfect passive* participle from a noun selected from the Exercise.
47. What *noun* in the Exercise is shortened by *poetic* license?
48. Define the *future perfect* tense.
49. Define a *preposition.* 50. Define *ellipsis*.

EXERCISES.

Synthesis.

1. Modify the subject of a simple sentence by *wise*.
2. Re-write the sentence expanding the adjective *wise* into an equivalent phrase.
3. Expand the phrase into an equivalent clause-modifier of the subject.
4. Write a sentence containing the adverb *silently*.
5. Expand this adverb into an equivalent phrase modifier of the predicate.
6. Write a sentence containing an infinitive of purpose.
7. Re-write the sentence expanding the infinitive into an equivalent clause.
8. Write two simple sentences about "*Grammar.*"
9. Properly combine these into a compound sentence.
10. Write a sentence containing a verb in the subjunctive without an *indicating* word.
11. Construct a negative-interrogative sentence having the verb in the past-perfect potential, passive.
12. Write a simple sentence in which *do* shall be *auxiliary* to itself.
13. Illustrate in a simple sentence the use of *had* as auxiliary.
14. Of *had* as principle verb.
15. Write a sentence containing a participial predicate adjective.

False Syntax.

1. The comparative degree can only be used with reference to two objects.   GOULD BROWN, p. 164.
2. Tell if the conjunctions are co-ordinate, subordinate, or correlative.   SWINTON'S GRAMMAR.
3. Wisdom or folly govern us.   FISK'S GRAMMAR.
4. When a verb governs a relative pronoun, it is placed after it.   CHAMBERS' GRAMMAR.
5. This mode of expression rather suits familiar than grave style.   MURRAY'S GRAMMAR.
6. A letter is a character that denotes one or more of the elementary sounds of language, and is the least distinct part of a written word.   KERL'S C. S. GRAMMAR, p. 35.

7. These rules should be kept in mind as aids either for speaking, composing, or parsing correctly. MORRELL'S GRAMMAR.

8. The Syntax and Etymology of the language is thus spread before the learner. BULLION'S GRAMMAR.

9. The passive Verb denotes Action received by the person or thing which is its Nominative. KIRKHAM'S GRAMMAR.

10. A noun or pronoun, used as the predicate of a proposition, is in the nominative case. HARVEY'S GRAMMAR.

---

11. I wish you would go back to the letter in which I told you of papa and me calling at Mr. Lemuel's. WM. BLACK.

12. It seemed that to waylay and murder the King and his brother was the shortest way. MACAULAY.

13. Have you seen anything of our friends since they left?
MAGAZINE.

14. Nor is it less pleased with its first successful endeavors to walk, or rather to run, which precedes walking. PALEY.

15. This kind of wit is that which abounds in Cowley, more than in any author that ever wrote. ADDISON.

EXERCISE XLIV.

1. "What is your name, my good woman?" asked he.
2. "Judith Gardenier."
3. "And your father's name?"
4. "Ah! poor man, Rip Van Winkle was his name, but it's
5. twenty years since he went away from home with his gun,
6. and never has been heard of since—his dog came home
7. without him; but whether he shot himself or was carried
8. away by the Indians, nobody can tell. I was then but a
9. little girl."
10. Rip had but one question more to ask; but he put it
11. with a faltering voice:
12. "Where's your mother?"
13. "Oh, she too had died but a short time since; she broke
14. a blood-vessel in a fit of passion at a New England peddler."
15. There was a drop of comfort, at least, in this intelligence.
16. The honest man could contain himself no longer. He
17. caught his daughter and her child in his arms. "I am
18. your father," cried he—"young Rip Van Winkle once—old
19. Rip Van Winkle now! Does nobody know poor Rip Van
20. Winkle?"

Washington Irving.

Analysis.

1. Classify the *first* sentence.
2. Give the *principal* proposition.
3. What is the syntax of the *dependent* clause?
4. Give the *subject-nominative* of "*is.*"
5. Classify "*what*" and state whether it has an antecedent.
6. Give the rule for parsing "*woman.*"

EXERCISES.

7. Write its possessive plural.
8. What is the syntax of *"Judith Gardenier"*?
9. Supply the *ellipsis* in the third line.
10. Classify the *fourth* sentence.
11. How many *propositions* has it?
12. Select from this sentence an *adverbial* clause.
13. A *substantive* clause.
14. A verb in the *present perfect* tense.
15. Is its nominative expressed or understood?
16. What *independent* words has this sentence?
17. Distinguish the difference between *"since"* in the *fifth* and in the *sixth* line.
18. Change *"I was then but a little girl"* to its corresponding *interrogative-negative* form.
19. Give the part of speech and syntax of *"but,"* line 8.
20. Give the *part of speech* and *syntactical* difference between the two *buts* in the ninth line.
21. Give the subject and the object of *"can tell."*
22. Give the *part of speech* and *syntax* of *"more."*
23. Give *mood* and *tense* of the verb in the same clause.
24. Classify the sentence comprising the thirteenth and fourteenth lines.
25-26. Write each verb of the sentence and give its subject and its object, if it has one.
27. Give the syntax of *"time."*
28. Of *"since,"* line 13.   29. Of *"too."*
30. What does *"in a fit of passion"* modify?
31. Classify *"there"* and give its syntactical use.
32. Classify *"at least,"* and state what it modifies.
33. Select from the extract an adverb, comparative degree.
34. How many *simple* sentences in the extract?
35. State the *syntactical* difference between "Rip Van Winkle," line 18, and the same, lines 19 and 20.
36. What is the syntax of *"in his arms"*?
37. What do *"once"* and *"now"* respectively modify?
38. Compare *"old,"* as applied to persons.
39. Select a verb in the *potential* mood and give its *synopsis* in that mood using your own name as subject.

EXERCISES. 141

40. Give all the participles, *active* and *passive*, of "*know.*"
41. Change the last sentence to its corresponding passive-declarative form.
42. What figure of *orthography* occurs in the twelfth line?
43. Select a simple word and form its *derivative*.
44. Give the opposite gender of "*daughter,*" and the possessive plural of "*child.*"
45. Classify "*w*" and "*y*" in "*away.*"
46. How many proper *diphthongal* sounds in the English language?
47. Select from the Exercise words to exemplify these sounds.
48. *Classify* and give the *syntax* of "*at least.*"
49. Define the *future perfect tense.*
50. Define the *present participle.*

Synthesis.

1. Write a complex sentence having an interrogative clause.
2. Write a complex sentence having an imperative clause.
3. Write a complex sentence whose clauses shall be connected by a relative pronoun in the *objective* case.
4. By a relative pronoun in the *possessive* case.
5. Write a sentence containing a clause in apposition with an objective noun.
6. Write a sentence containing an objective clause illustrating direct quotation.
7. Containing an appositive clause illustrating the same.
8. Change the latter to the form of *indirect* quotation.
9. Write a sentence having an adverbial clause of place and of time.
10. Write a sentence, introducing the subordinate clause by *whether*.
11. Write a sentence, connecting the two clauses by the correlatives *no sooner——than*.
12. Write a compound interrogative sentence with a dependent clause denoting time.
13. Write a complex sentence with a dependent clause denoting cause.
14. With a dependent clause denoting *purpose*.
15. Write a sentence having a *concessive clause.*

False Syntax.

1. Scott's works were, many of them, published in short intervals.
2. The committee was divided in their judgment.
3. We may be assured there was more discoverers than him.
4. He proposed to either largely decrease the appropriation or to do away wholly with it.
5. The merchants have on hand a large assortment of the latest styles, and are offered at the lowest prices.
6. Tell the gentleman, if he is in the hall, that I do not care to see him.
7. We must insist upon every man doing his duty.
8. I am very pleased to see you, Mr. Deronda[1]. GEO. ELIOT.
9.   My days are in the yellow leaf,
    The flower and fruit of life is gone.
10. I could heartily wish there was the same application and endeavors to cultivate and improve our church music as have been bestowed on that of the stage. ADDISON.

---

11. How jocund did they drive their team a-field.
12. Sailing up the river, the whole town may be seen.
13. There is an impenetrable veil between the visible and invisible world.
14. I was so tickled that I nearly died with laughter.
15. No one had exhibited the structure of the human kidneys; Vesalius had only examined them in dogs.

---

[1] Query as to whether the sentence is good English. The expression is frequently used by good writers.

EXERCISE XLV.

1. *Rom.* It is my love that calls upon my name!
2. How silver-sweet sound lovers' tongues by night,
3. Like softest music to attending ears!
4. *Jul.* Romeo!
5. *Rom.* My sweet!
6. *Jul.* At what o'clock to-morrow
7. Shall I send to thee?
8. *Rom.* At the hour of nine.
9. *Jul.* I will not fail; 'tis twenty years till then.
10. I have forgot why I did call thee back.
11. *Rom.* Let me stand here till thou remember it.
12. *Jul.* I shall forget, to have thee still stand there,
13. Rememb'ring how I love thy company.
14. *Rom.* And I'll still stay, to have thee still forget,
15. Forgetting any other home but this.
16. *Jul.* 'Tis almost morning; I would have thee gone
17. And yet no further than a wanton's bird;
18. Who lets it hop a little from her hand,
19. And with a silk thread plucks it back again,
20. So loving-jealous of its liberty.
21. *Rom.* I would I were thy bird.
22. *Jul.* Sweet, so would I!
23. Yet I should kill thee with much cherishing.
24. Good night, good night! Parting is such sweet sorrow
25. That I shall say—Good night, 'till it be morrow.

Shakespeare.

Analysis.

1. Classify the *first* sentence.
2. Name the first *compound* sentence.
3. Name the first *adjective* clause.
4. Name the first *substantive* clause.
5. Name the first *adverbial* clause.
6. What is the entire subject of the sentence beginning with "*I shall forget*"?
7. Give its *entire predicate*.
8. Should line 13 be classed as a *phrase* or as a *clause*?
9. Classify the sentence beginning with '*Tis almost morning.*"
10. Mention the *co-ordinate* clauses of this sentence.
11. What is the syntax of the clause "*who lets it hop*," &c.?
12. Classify the *last* sentence of the Exercise.
13. What is its *entire predicate?*
14–15. Give the syntax of each *subordinate* proposition.
16. Select an *imperative* sentence.
17. Select an *exclamatory* proposition.
18. Give the *mood* of "*remember."*

Classify and give the *syntax* of the following elements.

19. "*Silver-sweet*"; 20. "*by night*"; 21. "*Like*";
22. "*to attending ears*"; 23. "*At,*" line 6; 24. "*what*";
25. "*o'clock*"; 26. "*At the hour of nine*"; 27. "*then*";
28. "*why*"; 29. "*to have,*" line 12; 30. "*stand,*" line 12;
31. "*Forgetting*"; 32 "*how*"; 33. "*but*";
34. "*gone*"; 35. "*further*"; 36. "*bird,*" line 17;
37. "*hop*"; 38. "*little*"; 39. "*loving-jealous.*"

40. Give the *syntactical* difference between "*till,*" in the ninth line, and in the eleventh.
41. Of "*forget*" in the twelfth and in the fourteenth line.
42. Give the syntax of "*to have,*" line 14.
43. Classify "*sweet,*" line 5, and give the rule for parsing it.
44. Classify "*would*" in full, line 21.
45. Give its *object*, if transitive.
46. Give its *mood* and *tense*.
47. Give the *mood* and *tense* of "*were.*"

EXERCISES. 145

48. Parse "*night*," line 24.
49. What is the *syntactical* use of the expression, "*Good night*," last line?
50. Give the *mood* and *tense* of the last verb of the Exercise.

Synthesis.

1. Write a sentence containing an infinitive following *so——as*.
2. An infinitive following *than*.
3. An infinitive following *such*.
4. An infinitive as the object of a *participle*.
5. Write a sentence containing a *compound passive participle*.
6. A *present* participle, *transitive*, with a phrase-adjunct.
7. A compound passive participle as adjunct of a nominative-absolute.
8. Write a sentence containing a *complex* preposition.
9. Write a sentence containing an English idiom.
10. Write a sentence containing a *direct* and an *indirect* object.
11. Write three simple sentences about *trees*.
12. Correctly combine them into a compound sentence.
13. Write a complex sentence with the subordinate clause introduced by *when*.
14. Contract this sentence to a *simple* one by converting the dependent clause into a *nominative absolute with a participle*.
15. Write a *simple interrogative* sentence containing all the parts of speech.

False Syntax.

1. The hunter came into the room accompanied by his gun.
2. My uncle gave me not only the boat, but also taught me to row it.
3. They brought in the bouquets to the ladies in the evening in a large basket.
4. The first project was to shorten discourse by cutting polysyllables into one. SWIFT.
5. Such fruit is seldom or ever seen in this climate.
6. Who first discovered Martha's Vineyard? Gosnold, during 1602.

7. Seated on an upright tombstone, close to him, was a strange unearthly figure, whom Gabriel felt at once, was no being of this world. DICKENS.
8. We all went to the sea-shore for a little fresh air, from the city.
9. Nor want nor cold his course delay. DRYDEN.
10. Who would not have let them appeared? STEELE.
11. Were you not affrighted, and mistook your own shadow for the robber?
12. Thy beauty shines in Autumn unconfined,
And spreads a common feast for all that lives. THOMSON.
13. The sun looketh forth from the halls of the morning,
And flushes the clouds that begirt his career. W. G. CLARK.
14. I had as lief the town-crier spoke my lines. SHAKESPEARE.
15. A vision came before him as constant and more terrible than that from which he had escaped. DICKENS.

EXERCISE XLVI.

1. Some books are to be tasted, others to be swallowed,
2. and some few to be chewed and digested: that is, some
3. books are to be read only in parts; others to be read, but
4. not curiously; and some few to be read wholly, and with
5. diligence and attention. Some books also may be read by
6. deputy, and extracts made of them by others; but that
7. would be only in the less important arguments, and the
8. meaner sort of books; else distilled books are, like com-
9. mon distilled waters, flashy things. Reading maketh a
10. full man, conference a ready man, and writing an exact
11. man; and, therefore, if a man write little, he had need of
12. a great memory; if he confer little, he had need have a
13. present wit; and if he read little, he had need have much
14. cunning, to seem to know that he doth not. Histories
15. make men wise; poets, witty; the mathematics, subtle;
16. natural philosophy, deep; moral, grave; logic and rhetoric.
17. able to contend. *Bacon.*

Analysis.

1. State the number of sentences in the extract.
2. Classify each sentence.
3. How many *clauses* has the first sentence?
4. Has this sentence a *dependent* clause?
5. Give the syntax of "*to be swallowed.*"
6. Of "*to be chewed.*" 7. Of "*to be read.*"
8. Classify and give the *syntax* of "*that is.*"
9. Select a compound phrase from the first sentence.
10. Represent the phonetic spelling of "*philosophy.*"

Classify and give the *syntax* of the following elements:

11. "*Others,*" line 1; 12. "*few,*" line 2; 13. "*only,*" line 3;
14. "*but,*" line 3; 15. first "*and,*" line 4; 16. "*extracts*";
17. "*else*"; 18. "*things*"; 19. "*writing*";
20. "*and,*" line 11; 21. "*therefore*"; 22. "*if,*" line 11;
23. "*little,*" line 11; 24. "*to seem*"; 25. "*to know*";
26. "*that*"; 27. "*not,*" line 14; 28. "*poets*";
29. "*witty*"; 30. "*to contend.*"

31. *Name* and *classify* the *second* predicate-verb, line 11.
32. Give its *mood* and *tense*.
33. Name the predicate-verb in "*he had need have much cunning.*"
34. Give its *mood* and *tense*.
35. *Classify* and give *syntax* of "*have*" in same sentence.
36. Why is "*to*" not expressed before "*have*"?
37. What part of speech immediately precedes "*have*"?
38. Name all the *adverbial* clauses of the extract.
39. Name a *substantive* clause.
40. What words *might* be used instead of "*had,*" line 11?
41. Name all the verbs in the *subjunctive* mood.
42. Name those in the *potential* mood.
43. Mention a case of "*false syntax,*" if there is one, in the Exercise, and correct the error.
44. Give the rule for doubling the "*l*" in "*distilled.*
45. Why is "*writing*" not spelled *writeing*?
46. Select a noun having the same form for either number.

47. Mention four words in the extract each having a *silent* consonant.

48. Change "*histories make men wise*" to the other tense forms, *passive*, of the same mood.

49. Define *pleonasm*. 50. Define *enallage*.

Synthesis.

1. Write a simple sentence containing three prepositions.
2. Write a complex sentence with an adjective clause connected by a conjunctive adverb.
3. Write a compound sentence containing an interrogative and an imperative clause.
4. Containing a declarative and an interrogative clause.
5. Write a sentence that shall illustrate the figure *enallage*.
6. Compose two simple sentences and one complex sentence about *rivers*.
7. Combine these into a compound sentence.
8. Write a sentence containing an *adverb of manner*.
9. Re-write the sentence expanding the *adverb* into a manner phrase.
10. Write a sentence in which "*and*" shall connect a word and a phrase.
11. Write a complex sentence having a relative pronoun whose antecedent is a *possessive* pronoun.
12. Write a complex sentence properly using the words, *should* and *would*.
13. A present participle as a predicate adjective.
14. A perfect participle as a predicate adjective.
15. Write a sentence containing a word illustrating the rule for *doubling* the *final consonant*.

False Syntax.

1. I think if I am not mistaken that you are wrong.
2.   It is not fit for such as us
        To sit with rulers of the land.   SCOTT.
3. It was remarked by Noah Webster that he had never ventured to coin but one word.   HAVEN'S RHETORIC.

4. A large stock of these short words are understood by nearly all who speak the English language, and are first learned by children.
ID.

5. Both minister and magistrate is compelled to choose between his duty and his reputation. JUNIUS.

6. The richness of her arms and apparel were conspicuous in the foremost ranks. GIBBON.

7. These (the commas) are inserted by the compositors without the slightest compunction. DEAN ALFORD.

8. In all abstract cases where we merely speak of numbers the verb is better singular. ID.

9. The farmer after having fallen the tree, found it had fell upon a setting hen that had lain her eggs under its branches.

10. Channing's mind was planted as thick with thoughts as a back wood of his own magnificent land.

---

11. We have now a new school house in the town large enough to hold four hundred pupils, three stories high.

12. He then addressed the crowds who were returning from the riot.

13. Where all must fall or not coherent be,
And all that rises, rise in due degree. POPE.

14. She began to extol the farmer's, as she called him, excellent understanding.

15. At the crossing, my foot slipped, and I pretty near fell down.

EXERCISE XLVII.

1. Besides, naturally speaking, a man bids fairer for great-
2. ness of soul who is the descendant of worthy ancestors
3. and has good blood in his veins, than one who is come of an
4. ignoble and obscure parentage. For these reasons, I think
5. a man of merit who is derived from an illustrious line is
6. very justly to be regarded more than a man of equal
7. merit who has no claim to hereditary honors. * * * *
8. My Lord Froth has been so educated in punctilio that
9. he governs himself by a certain ceremonial in all the ordi-
10. nary occurrences of life. He measures out his bow to the
11. degree of the person he converses with. I have seen him
12. in every inclination of the body, from a familiar nod to
13. the low stoop in the salutation sign. I remember five of
14. us who were acquainted with one another, met together
15. one morning at his lodgings, when a wag in the company
16. was saying it would be worth while to observe how he
17. would distinguish us at his first entrance. Accordingly,
18. he had no sooner come into the room, but casting his eye
19. about, "My Lord Such-a-one," says he, "your most hum-
20. ble servant. Sir Richard, your humble servant. Your
21. servant, Mr. Ironside. Mr. Ducker, how do you do?
22. Hah! Frank, are you there?"

Addison.

Analysis.

1. How many *sentences* in the above selection?
2. Classify the *first* sentence.
3. Give its *entire* subject.
4. Give its *entire* predicate.
5. Select from this sentence the *adverbial* clause, and state what it modifies.

EXERCISES. 151

6. What *correlative* words occur in the first sentence?
7. Give the *part of speech* and *syntactical* office of "*besides*"?
8. Of "*speaking.*" 9. Of "*fairer.*" 10. Of "*one,*" line 3.
11. Is "*is come*" in the *passive* voice?
12. Give all the modifiers of "*man,*" line 1.
13. Classify the *second* sentence.
14. Mention its *principal* clause.
15. Give the *simple subject* and *predicate* of each *dependent* clause.
16. Has "*for these reasons*" a conjunctive force?
17. What *word* might be appropriately substituted for this phrase?
18. What *correlative connectives* occur in the second sentence?
19. Give the *part of speech* of *each* of them.
20. What is the object of "*think*"?
21. Classify the *third* sentence.
22. Name its *correlative* words.
23. Of what *part of speech* are these *correlatives*?
24. Give the *subject-nominative* of the principal clause.
25. Give the *mood, tense,* and *form* of its *predicate-verb.*
26. Classify the *fourth* sentence.
27. Give its *dependent* clause and state whether this clause is *adjective* or *adverbial* in office.
28. Give the *connective* and state its *full* syntactical office.
29. What is the *syntax* of "*from a familiar nod*"?
30. Classify the sentence beginning with "*I remember.*"
31. Of how many *subordinate* clauses does it consist?
32-36. Give the *simple subject* and *predicate* of each.
37. Give the *part of speech* and *syntax* of "*worth.*"
38. Of "*while.*" 39. Of "*to observe.*" 40. Of "*when.*"
41. Classify the sentence beginning with "*accordingly.*"
42. Give the *part of speech* and *syntax* of "*accordingly.*"
43. Of "*but.*" 44. Of "*casting.*" 45. Of "*Such-a-one.*"
46. Of "*servant,*" line 20.
47. Mention the *correlative* words of this sentence and give their *part of speech*.
48. Correct this sentence, if faulty in any respect.
49. Which "*do*" is *auxiliary*?
50. Define *punctuation*.

EXERCISES.

Synthesis.

1. Write a sentence in which the entire predicate shall comprise all the words *expressed* in the sentence.
2. Write a sentence containing three nouns denoting joint possession.
3. Denoting separate possession.
4. Write a sentence containing all the *cases*, including the nominative independent and the nominative absolute.
5. An adjective belonging to a subject-phrase.
6. An adjective belonging to a subject-clause.
7. Write a sentence containing a participle used as a pure adverb.
8. An adjective comparing two nouns as to some quality possessed by both.
9. An adjective relating to an adjective and a noun as one compound term.
10. Write a sentence containing a verb in the imperative mood, first person plural. (Need not be original.)
11. Write a sentence illustrating *poetic license*.
12. Illustrating a figure of Orthography.
13. A figure of Syntax.
14. A figure of Rhetoric.
15. Write a sentence containing an *illative* clause modified by a *conditional* clause.

False Syntax.

1. A's income is equal to half of B's, which is a thousand dollars.
2. A servant will obey a master's orders whom he loves.
3. This dedication may serve for almost any book that has, is, or shall be published.
4. Literary and scientific men hastened to the court of Charlemagne, anxious to secure the favor of the greatest monarch of his age.
5. We rested beneath the umbrageous shadow of a shady oak, and then again resumed our journey anew.
6. We informed him of the difficulty, that he may be prepared for it.
7. He made some comments where too much personalities were indulged in.

8. Hadn't she ought to mention the antecedent? MANY PUPILS.
9. We cannot doubt but that the undertaking will succeed.
MAGAZINE.
10. Unfortunately, this institution has had no endorsement, as it should have. ROCHESTER PAPER.

11.   My hair is gray but not with years,
            Nor grew it white
          In a single night
       As men's have done from sudden fears.   BYRON.

12. Whom none but Heaven and you and I shall hear.
13. The lady sits a horse with exceeding grace.
14. They flew to arms and attacked the Duke of Northumberland's horse whom they put to death. HUME.
15. I have noticed that the Bible is always particular to never refer to even the illustrious mother of mankind herself as "a lady," but speaks of her as a *woman*. MARK TWAIN.

EXERCISE XLVIII.

1. It was in his thirteenth year that the family removed to
2. that better church-living at Schwarzenbach; with which
3. change, so far as school education was concerned, pros-
4. pects considerably brightened for him. The public teacher
5. there was no deep scholar or thinker, yet a lively, genial
6. man, and warmly interested in his pupils; among whom
7. he soon learned to distinguish Fritz, as a boy of altogether
8. superior gifts. What was of still more importance, Fritz
9. now got access to books; entered into a course of highly
10. miscellaneous, self-selected reading; and what with ro-
11. mances, what with Belles-letters works, and Huchesonian
12. philosophy, and controversial divinity, saw an astonish-
13. ing scene opening round him on all hands. His Latin
14. and Greek were now better taught; he even began learn-
15. ing Hebrew. Two clergymen of the neighborhood took
16. pleasure in his company young as he was; and were of
17. great service now and afterwards; it was under their
18. auspices that he commenced composition, and also specu-
19. lating on theology, wherein he inclined strongly to the
20. heterodox side.

Carlyle, on Richter.

Analysis.

1. Classify the *first* sentence of the selection.
2. Select a *dependent* clause from this sentence.
3. Is this clause *adjective* or *adverbial* in office? and what does it modify?

EXERCISES.

4. Give the *syntax* of "*with which change.*"
5. Give the *syntax* of "*so far as school education was concerned.*"
6. Of "*so far as.*"
7. Give the *syntax* of each word in the above conjunctive phrase.
8. Give the simple predicate of "*education.*"
9. Classify the *second* sentence.
10. How many *propositions* has it?
11. Give the *syntax* of the *last* clause of this sentence.
12. Give the *part of speech* and the *syntax* of "*there.*"
13. Of "*no.*" 14. Of "*thinker.*" 15. Of "*yet.*"
16. Of "*man.*" 17. Of "*interested.*" 18. Of "*to distinguish.*"
19. Of "*as,*" line 7. 20. Of "*boy.*" 21. Of "*altogether.*"
22. Give the *syntax* of "*among whom.*"
23. Classify the *third* sentence.
24. Give the *syntax* of its *first* clause.
25. How many *clauses* has this sentence?
26. *Classify* and give the *syntax* of "*what,*" line 8.
27. Of "*still.*" 28. Of "*entered.*" 29. Of "*and,*" line 10.
30. Of "*what,*" line 11. 31. Of "*Huchesonian.*"
32. Of "*with,*" line 11. 33. Of "*Belles-lettres.*" 34. Of "*divinity.*"
35. Of "*saw.*" 36. Of "*on all hands.*"
37. Classify the *fourth* sentence.
38. Give the subject and the object of "*began.*"
39. Classify the *last* sentence.
40. How many *propositions* are contained in this sentence?
41. Classify and give the *syntax* of '*young as he was.*"
42. Give the *part of speech* and the *syntax* of "*young.*"
43. Of "*as.*" 44. Of "*afterwards.*"
45. Give the *syntax* of the clause "*that he commenced composition.*"
46. What is the *syntax* of the *last* clause of the Exercise?
47. What is the *part of speech* and the *syntax* of "*wherein*"?
48. Select from the Exercise a noun modified by a *participle*, and by a *participial* adjective.
49. *Classify* and give the *syntax* of "*speculating.*"
50. What parts of speech neither *modify*, nor are *modified*?

Synthesis.

1. Write a sentence containing the sign *to* of the infinitive, *omitted* after the present participle.
2. A sentence having an infinitive used as a modifier of a participle.
3. Write sentences illustrating *far*, as an *adjective*, as an *adverb*, and as a *noun*.
4. Illustrate the same with *like*.
5. Write a sentence containing an infinitive, a participle, and a noun made proper by personification.
6. A clause expressive of *purpose* (or *end*), modified by an adverbial clause of place.
7. Write a sentence containing a *direct* quotation.
8. An *indirect* quotation.
9. Write a sentence containing the expletive *there*.
10. Write a sentence having a compound progressive participle.
11. An interrogative clause in the nominative case.
12. An interrogative clause in apposition.
13. Write a sentence containing a relative pronoun of four syllables.
14. Write a complex sentence of two clauses connected by *or else*.
15. Write a sentence containing an *adversative* clause.

False Syntax.

1. They returned back again to the city from whence they came forth.
2. Had they intended to have returned, they would have been here before now.
3. The language with which Rask was dealing was one of all others wherein the difference in question required to be accurately drawn.
Dr. Latham.

4. Did you observe the moon's appearance last night to be any different than usual?
Newspaper.

5. "I am far from a very inquisitive man by temperament," said Kenelm.
Bulwer.

6. I do not remember that I ever spoke three sentences together in my life.
Spectator.

7. At this point the party met with quite an unexpected accident.
A Novel.

8. " 'Got any luck?' says I. 'No,' says he. 'Well,' says I, 'I've got the finest string of trouts ever was seen.' "
Cited in GILMORE'S "ART OF EXPRESSION."

9. I am so much surprised by this statement that I am desirous of resigning, that I scarcely know what reply to make.
Cited in ABBOTT'S "HOW TO WRITE CLEARLY."

10. But that did him no more good than his afterward trying to pacify the Barons with lies.
DICKENS.

11. Since he, miscalled the morning star,
  Nor man nor fiend hath fallen so far. BYRON.

12. The evidences of sin and vice are seen all about me.
A FASTIDIOUS YOUNG LADY.

13. I shall supply you with money now, and I will furnish you with a reasonable sum from time to time, on your application to me by letter.
GEO. ELIOT, *Middlemarch*.

14. We are at peace with all the world, and seek to maintain our cherished relations of amity with the rest of mankind.
PRESIDENT TAYLOR.

15. He loved the boy so dearly, and alas! he loved him not.
SEAFORTH.

EXERCISE XLIX.

1. (a). Hampden, with his head drooping, and his hands
2. leaning on his horse's neck, moved feebly out of the
3. battle. The mansion which had been inhabited by his
4. (b). father-in-law and from which in his youth he had car-
5. ried home his bride, Elizabeth, was in sight. There
6. (c). still remains an affecting tradition, that he looked for a
7. moment toward that beloved house, and made an effort
8. to go thither to die.
9. (d). The news of Hampden's death produced as great a
10. consternation in his party, according to Clarendon, as
11. if their whole army had been cut off. The journals of
12. (e). the time amply prove that the Parliament and all its
13. friends were filled with grief and dismay. Lord Nugent
14. (f). has quoted a remarkable passage from the next *Weekly*
15. *Intelligencer*. " The loss of Colonel Hampden goeth
16. near the heart of every man that loves the good of his
17. (g). king and his country; and makes some conceive little
18. content to be at the army now that he has gone. The
19. (h). memory of this deceased colonel is such that in no age
20. to come but it will more and more be had in honor and
21. esteem; a man so religious, and of that prudence, judg-
22. ment, temper, valor, and integrity, that he hath left
23. few his like behind him." *Macaulay.*

Analysis.

1. How many *simple* sentences in the above selection?
2. How many *complex* sentences?
3. Give the *entire* subject of sentence (*a*).
4. Give the *entire* subject of sentence (*b*).
5. Select a noun *antecedent* to two relative pronouns.
6. Classify sentence (*c*). 7. Give its *principal* clause.

8. What is the *syntactical* difference between the two "*thats*"?
9. Give the modifiers of "*tradition.*"
10. What is the *syntax* of "*to die*"?
11. Classify sentence (*d*). 12. Give its *entire predicate*.
13. Give the *syntactical* office of its dependent clause.
14. Parse the *connective*.
15. Give the *syntax* of "*according to Clarendon.*"
16. Give the gender of "*army.*" 17. Classify sentence (*e*).
18. Give the points in which its two verbs *correspond*.
19. Give the *synopsis* of the verb in line 13.
20. Classify sentence (*f*). 21. Classify sentence (*g*).
22-23. Give the *syntax* of its two dependent clauses.
24. Mention the *connective* of the *last* one.
25. Classify sentence (*h*) 26. Give its *entire predicate*.
27. Give the *syntax* of the clause immediately following "*but.*"
28. Is the *last* clause *adjective* or *adverbial* in office, and on what does it depend?
29. Name the *last preposition* of sentence (*a*) and state what it connects.
30. Give the *part of speech* and the *syntax* of "*leaning.*"
31. Of "*home.*" 32. Of "*Elizabeth.*" 33. Of "*thither.*"
34. Give the *third preposition* in sentence (*d*) and state what it connects.
35. What is the *syntax* of "*their whole army had been cut off,*" and *by* what and *to* what is this clause connected?
36. *Classify* and give the *syntax* of "*conceive.*"
37. Of "*now.*" 38. Of "*such.*" 39. Of "*but.*" 40. Of "*man.*"
41. Parse the *adverb* in line 20.
42. What *correlative* words occur in the last sentence?
43. Give the possessive plural of the feminine of "*father-in-law.*"
44. What *comparative* clause might be supplied in sentence (*d*)?
45. How do "*party* and "*Parliament*" differ with respect to *gender*?
46. Classify "*like,*" and give its *syntax*.
47. What does "*and*" connect, line 21?
48. Give the *syntax* of "*in no age to come.*"
49. Correct any portion of the Exercise that may not be conformable with *present* usage.
50. Define *Personification*.

Synthesis.

1. Write a complex sentence containing five clauses.
2. Write a sentence having four independent clauses, one interrogative.
3. Having a noun-clause in the objective case.
4. Write a sentence containing an *alternative* clause.
5. A *copulative* clause with the connective understood.
6. An *adversative* clause connected by some conjunction other than *but*.
7. An *illative* or *inferential* clause.
8. Write a sentence containing a *nominative absolute* before a participle.
9. A *nominative absolute* after a participle.
10. Expand the *absolute phrase* of question 8 into a clause.
11. Write a simple sentence containing an adjective and an adverb, each in the superlative degree.
12. Write a complex sentence having six prepositions, two of them being understood.
13. Write a complex sentence containing a *simple*, a *complex*, and a *compound* phrase.
14. Containing *which* as an *adjective*.
15. Containing a *prepositional*, a *participial*, and an *independent* phrase.

False Syntax.

1. The genii who was expected to be present was deaf to every call.
2. I like Hawthorne better than Irving's style.
3. He then got into the carriage to sit with the man whom he had been told was Morgan.
4. I had studied grammar previous to his instructing me, but to no purpose.
5. Did you never bear false witness against thy neighbor?
 DRAPER.
6. Neither of these two definitions do rightly adjust the genuine signification of this tense. JOHNSON'S GRAMMAR.
7. One can scarce help smiling at the blindness of a certain critic.
 KAMES.

8. { They were within three miles from Kinston.   N. Y. HERALD.
   { These papers I have not incorporated in the present volume.
                                    SWINTON, *Rambles among Words.*

9. It is the business of an epic poet to copy after nature.   BLAIR.

10.   Man feels his weakness, and to numbers run
        Himself to strengthen, or himself to shun.   CRABBE.

---

11.   My robe and my integrity to heaven
        Is all I dare now call my own.   SHAKSPERE.

12.   Early to bed, and early to rise,
        Makes a man healthy, wealthy, and wise.   FRANKLIN.

13. With a freedom more like a milk-maid of the town than she of the plains, she accosted him.   SCOTT, as quoted in Hill's Rhetoric.

14. The returns, official and otherwise, foot up as follows.
                                    THACKERAY: ID.

15. We have the power of ascertaining, altering, and compounding those images which we have received, into all the varieties of picture and vision.   WEBSTER.

EXERCISE L.

I.

1. And therefore, first of all, I tell you earnestly and author-
2. itatively (I *know* I am right in this), you must get into the
3. habit of looking intensely at words, and assuring yourself
4. of their meaning, syllable by syllable,—nay, letter by letter.
5. * * * If you read ten pages of a good book, letter by
6. letter,—that is to say, with real accuracy,—you are for
7. evermore in some measure an educated person. * * *
8. A well educated gentleman may not know many languages
9. —may have read very few books. But whatever language
10. he knows, he knows precisely; whatever word he pro-
11. nounces, he pronounces rightly; above all he is learned in
12. the *peerage* of words; knows the words of true descent and
13. ancient blood, at a glance, from words of modern canaille;
14. remembers all their ancestry, their intermarriages, distant
15. relationship, and offices they held at any time and in any
16. country. *Ruskin in Sesame and Lilies.*

II.

1. "It's only our sister, Joseph," said Amelia laughing,
2. and shaking the two fingers which he held out. "I've
3. come home for good, you know; and this is my friend,
4. Miss Sharp, whom you have heard me mention." "No,
5. never, upon my word," said the head under the neck-cloth,
6. shaking very much,—"that is, yes,—what abominably
7. cold weather, Miss;"—and herewith he fell to poking the
8. fire with all his might, although it was in the middle of
9. June. *Thackeray in Vanity Fair.*

Analysis.

FIRST EXTRACT.

1. Classify the *first* sentence.
2. How many *propositions* has it?
3. Give the *predicate-verb* of each of its principal propositions.
4. Give the *simple* subject and predicate of each subordinate clause.
5. What is the *object* of the verb "*tell*"?
6. What is the *syntax* of "*I am right in this*"?
7. Give the *modifiers* of "*habit.*"   8. Of "*assuring.*"
9. Give the *syntax* of *first* "*syllable,*" line 4.
10. Give the *part of speech* and the *syntax* of "*nay.*"
11. What is the *syntactical* office of "*letter by letter*"?
12. Classify the *second* sentence.
13. How many *clauses* has it?
14. Which clause is *principal*?
15. What *modifiers* has "*read*"?
16. Give its *mood* and *tense.*
17. Give the *syntactical* office of "*that is to say*"?
18. Is this clause *dependent,* or *independent*?
19. *Classify* and give the *syntax* of "*to say.*"
20. Is the *subject* of "*may have read*" *expressed,* or *understood*?
21. Classify the *last* sentence.
22. How many *propositions* has it?
23. How many *subordinate* propositions has it?
24. Classify these propositions (if you find more than one) as to whether they are *adjective* or *adverbial* in office.
25. Give the *object* of each verb in line 10.
26. How are the first two clauses of the last sentence connected?
27. *Classify* and give the *syntax* of "*whatever.*"
28. Of "*above all.*"
29. Give the object of "*held,*" if it has one.
30. What is the *syntax* of the *first* "*he knows*"?
31. Select a *simple,* a *complex,* and a *compound* phrase, from the last sentence and state what each modifies.
32. Give the *part of speech* and the *syntax* of "*evermore.*"
33. Represent the spelling of "*language*" by its *elementary* sounds.

SECOND EXTRACT.

34. Classify the *first* sentence.
35. Give the *entire subject* of this sentence.
36. Give the *syntax* of its *subordinate* clauses.
37. Classify the *second* sentence.
38. Give the *syntax* of each of its *modifying* clauses.
39. By what is *"friend"* modified?
40. Classify the *third* sentence.
41. How many clauses has it, *expressed,* or *understood?*
42. *Classify* and give the *syntax* of *"never."*
43. Of *"upon my word."*
44. Of *"that is."* 45. Of *"weather."*
46. Parse *"no,"* and *"yes."*
47. Give the *modifiers* of *"head."*
48. State the precise difference between a participial, and an infinitive-noun, as to the modifiers each may take.
49. What figure of Rhetoric is found in the proposition *"said the head under the neck-cloth"?*
50. State the difference between a *simile* and a *metaphor*, and exemplify each.

Synthesis.

1. Write a sentence containing only the parts of speech that *may be modified*, each having a modifier in the sentence given.
2. Write a sentence having an *imperative* and an *interrogative* clause.
3. An adverbial clause expressing *purpose.*
4. Abridge the sentence last formed, by changing the subordinate clause into an *infinitive of purpose.*
5. Change the adverbial clause of *"as we passed up the river, we viewed the beautiful landscape"* to its equivalent participial construction.
6. Write a complex *exclamatory* sentence.
7. A complex *interrogative* sentence.
8. Write a sentence in which the preposition *for* has no antecedent term of relation.

9. Write a sentence denoting comparison of equality as applied to the adjective *beautiful*.

10. One of inequality applied to the adjective *wise*.

11. Change the substantive clause of "*that one should prove false to his friend, is base,*" to an equivalent infinitive construction.

12. Write a sentence containing a substantive phrase modified by an *adjective*.

13. A *prepositional* phrase modified by an *adverb*.

14. Expand into a *concessive* clause the italicized phrase in the sentence, "*In spite of great opposition*, the man will succeed."

15. Write a compound sentence having an *adverbial* clause of *time*, of *manner*, and of *place*, together with an *adjectival*, an *adverbial*, and a *substantive* phrase.

False Syntax.

1. I write these lines while waiting in a refreshment room at Reading between a Great Western and a South Eastern train.
DEAN ALFORD.

2. "Ah, Mr. F.," replied Mr. Irving," you are greatly mistaken," and taking down some of his MSS., he showed it to him full of erasures and interlineations. THE YOUTH'S COMPANION.

3. Secluded and alone, he now partook of his solitary repast, which he entirely consumed. NOVEL.

4. King Harrold, wounded with an arrow in the eye, was nearly blind. DICKENS.

5. The sailor and child, who was a fine little fellow of about nine years old, now came into the room. CHATTERBOX.

6. Finding escape impossible, she threw her feather-bed out on the ground, and grasping her two children, leaped from the second story window upon it. All then escaped unhurt. WESTERN JOURNAL.

7. There is not a girl in town, but, let her have her will in going to a mask, and she shall dress like a shepherdess. ADDISON.

8. I simply read the extract to show that my *ipse dixit* need not be taken. A PRINCIPAL.

9. "Well, farmer, then let's you and I go by ourselves." And while he hesitated, the lady asked him was he come to finish the bust.
From "PUT YOURSELF IN HIS PLACE."

10. Two other words occur to me which are very commonly mangled by our clergy. One of these is *covetous*, and its substantive *covetousness*. I hope some who read these lines, will be induced to leave off pronouncing them *covetious* and *covetiousness*. I can assure them that when they do thus call them, one at least of their hearers has his appreciation of their teaching disturbed.

DEAN ALFORD'S " PLEA FOR THE QUEEN'S ENGLISH."

Mr. Moon, the Dean's critic, maintains that the above sentence is capable of 10240 different meanings.

11. As a text-book, the volume has one technical defect,—the lines ought to have been numbered either as in the other volumes or on each page. Its absence is a source of annoyance.

THE NATION: *Cited in Hill's Rhetoric.*

12. The Board offer their grateful acknowledgments for the liberal support hitherto so freely extended, and which has so greatly contributed to this satisfactory result.

Cited in DEAN ALFORD'S "THE QUEEN'S ENGLISH."

13. A husband, on receiving news of the sudden and violent death of a lady in whom he had so near an interest, might have been expected to have at least gone in person to the spot. FROUDE.

14. The Bishop of Ross undertook that his mistress would do anything which the Queen of England and the nobility desired. IBID.

15. The teacher said, in speaking of that that, that that that that that pupil parsed was not the that that that visitor requested him to analyze.

THE END.

www.ingramcontent.com/pod-product-compliance
Lightning Source LLC
Chambersburg PA
CBHW030251170426
43202CB00009B/700